Contemplating the Trinity

The Path to the Abundant Christian Life

Contemplating the Trinity

The Path to the Abundant Christian Life

Raniero Cantalamessa, OFM Cap

Translated by Marsha Daigle-Williamson, PhD

English language edition copyright © 2007 by Raniero Cantalamessa, OFM Cap
First published in Italian under the title, *Contemplando la Trinità,* by Ancora
Editrice, Milan, Italy, copyright © 2002 by Ancora S.r.l.
All rights reserved

The Word Among Us Press
9639 Doctor Perry Road
Ijamsville, Maryland 21754
www.wordamongus.org

11 10 09 08 07 2 3 4 5 6

ISBN: 978-1-59325-097-3

Cover design by DesignWorks Group
Cover image: Rublev, Andrei (1360–c.1430)
Icon of the Old Testament Trinity, c.1410
Tretyakov Gallery, Moscow, Russia
Scala / Art Resource, NY

Made and printed in the United States of America

Library of Congress Cataloging-in-Publication Data

Cantalamessa, Raniero.
[Contemplando la Trinità. English]
Contemplating the Trinity : the path to the abundant Christian life / Raniero
Cantalamessa ; translated by Marsha Daigle-Williamson.
  p. cm.
Includes bibliographical references.
ISBN 978-1-59325-097-3 (alk. paper)
1. Trinity. 2. Christian life--Catholic authors. I. Title.
BT111.3.C3613 2007
231'.044--dc22
          2006036642

Table of Contents

Preface

This book contains a series of meditations given at the papal household during Advent of 2000, the Jubilee Year, and in Lent of 2001, the first year of the new millennium. This completes the series of books on the mysteries of Christ in the life of the church, which includes the mystery of the nativity, the baptism of Christ, the transfiguration, the word of God, Easter, and Pentecost. The Trinity is also a mystery "of Christ" in that he was the one who revealed it to us and is himself part of it.

In his apostolic letter *Novo millennio ineunte*, Pope John Paul II speaks of a "high standard" for Christian holiness, and I have attempted to demonstrate how the Trinity itself is that high standard. I have applied the exciting invitation that resounds in that letter—*Duc in altum*, "launch out into the deep"—to the Trinity, because I am convinced of the need for a breath of fresh air, a new perspective on Christian life, that is more clearly trinitarian. The Trinity is the "bottomless sea without shores" in which Christ invites us to immerse ourselves in everything he continually says about the Father and the Spirit in the gospel.

I was encouraged to take these reflections out of the halls of the papal household by the kindness of the supreme pontiff, who heard these reflections and often asked me to give him the texts to reread. I was also moved by the conviction some cardinals expressed to me that these reflections could help develop a trinitarian spirituality, which the church sees a growing need for, among laypeople as well. All important events and acts of Christianity begin in the name of the Trinity, so it is appropriate for the new millennium to begin this way: in the name of the Father, the Son, and the Holy Spirit.

Given my frequent references to a few famous artistic representations of the Trinity, four colored illustrations have been included to encourage the contemplation of the mystery, as is the nature of icons.

Chapter 1

Contemplating the Trinity "to Overcome the Hateful Divisions of This World"[1]:

THE TRINITY IN EASTERN SPIRITUALITY

1. The Icon of the Trinity by Andrej Rublëv

To get to the heart of Eastern and Western spirituality, we can take as our starting point the artistic representation of the Trinity that is the most typical for each of the two churches.

For the Orthodox Church, that would certainly be Rublëv's icon of the Trinity. Painted in 1425 for the church of St. Sergius and preserved today in the Tretyakov Gallery in Moscow, this icon was declared to be the model for all representations of the Trinity in 1551 by the Council of 100 Chapters.

One thing should be said immediately about this icon. It does not purport to directly represent the Trinity, which is, by definition, invisible and ineffable. Attempting to do so would be contrary to all the canons of Byzantine ecclesiastical iconography. Instead, it depicts the three angels who appeared to Abraham by the oaks of Mamre (see Genesis 18:1-15). In that tradition, before and after Rublëv, Abraham, Sarah, the calf, and an oak tree often appear. This episode, in fact, is read by the patristic tradition as an early prefigurement of the Trinity. The icon is one of the artistic forms that follow a spiritual reading of the Bible. It is, thus, not the atemporal Trinity that is represented, but the Trinity in salvation history.

All the experts agree that Rublëv's icon is the zenith of all iconographic art in terms of its power for theological synthesis, its richness of symbols, and its artistic beauty. It conveys the very rhythm of trinitarian life.[2] Unceasing motion and superhuman stillness, transcendence and condescendence, are simultaneously represented.

The dogma of the unity and trinity of God is expressed by the fact that the three Persons represented are distinct but closely resemble each other. They are contained within a circle that highlights their unity, but their diverse motions and postures speak of their differences.

In the original, all three are wearing blue garments as a sign of the divine nature they have in common. But on top of or underneath the blue garments, each one has a distinctive color: the Father, the angel to the left, has an indefinable color almost of pure light as a sign of his invisibility and inaccessibility. The Son, in the center, is wearing a dark tunic as a sign of the humanity with which he has clothed himself. The Holy Spirit, the angel to the right, wears a green mantle as a sign of life, since he is "the one who gives life."

Lengthy contemplation of this icon can yield more insight into the Trinity than reading whole treatises on it. The icon is a window that opens out to the invisible, through which the first flashes of eternal life reach us. Rublëv must have meditated for a long time on the words of Gregory Nazianzus, whom the Orthodox brothers call "the cantor of the Trinity":

Long ago I tore my spirit from the world and mingled it with the shining spirits of heaven. The lofty mind bore me far from the flesh, set me in that place, and hid me in the recesses of the heavenly abode. There the light of the Trinity shone upon my eyes. . . . It is throned on high and gives off an ineffable and harmonious radiance. . . . I died to the world and the world to me. . . . [3]

One thing is especially striking as we contemplate Rublëv's icon: the profound peace and unity that emanate from the whole. A silent cry comes forth from the icon: "Be one as we are one." The saint for whose monastery the icon was painted, St. Sergius of Radonezh, is known in Russian history for having brought unity among warring chieftains and for having thus made possible the liberation of Russia from the Tartars, who had invaded it. His motto was that "through the contemplation of the most Holy Trinity we can overcome the hateful divisions of this world." Rublëv wanted to make use of the spiritual inheritance of this great saint who had made the Trinity the fundamental inspiration for his life and work.

2. Unity: Departure or Arrival Point?

The Eastern vision of the Trinity is above all, then, a call to unity. At first sight, this could appear to contrast with what we know of Greek and Latin theologies. It is well known that in discussions of the Trinity, the Greeks and Latins went in opposite directions: the Greeks began with the divine Persons, that is, from plurality, and proceeded to nature and thus to unity; the Latins, on the other hand, began with nature, or divine unity, and proceeded to the Persons.[4] With the Latins, unity led to plurality, and with the Greeks, plurality led to unity. In the Latin vision, this characterization is clearly confirmed by the fact that the treatment of divine unity in Western theology—the *De Deo uno* ("concerning the oneness of God")—precedes the treatment of divine plurality, the *De Deo trino* ("concerning the triune nature of God").

It would thus seem more logical to receive a call to unity from the Latin vision rather than the Greek one. However, there is a profound reason to do just the opposite. In the Latin vision the unity occurs at the beginning, while in the Greek vision unity is the point of arrival, so to speak. In this respect, it is more similar to the unity that needs to be experienced by people in the church and in the world. Unity is not a given for us that we need to keep intact through changing circumstances; it is a goal we are always trying to restore. The fundamental fact in the church is that we are diverse members, with diverse gifts; but, "though many," we are called to form "one body" (see Romans 12:5).

The different visions of the Trinity are reflected in the way the church is seen in the East and in the West. This is worth emphasizing, because it can help reinforce the desire and necessity for full unity between them. For those in the East, the plurality of the churches is an assumption that is taken for granted. The problem, or challenge, is how to ensure an effective and efficacious unity undergirding the autonomy of the individual churches. It is just the opposite for the Catholic Church: unity is the strongest and most obvious assumption, guaranteed by the exercise of the primacy by Peter's successor. The problem, or challenge, is how to allow the required room for diversity, i.e., for the pluralism and autonomy of the local churches. In the East, pluralism is the departure point and unity is the goal; for the West, unity is the departure point and plurality is the goal. The same is true of their respective trinitarian doctrines: the pitfall for the Latins to avoid has always been *Monarchianism*, i.e., excessive insistence on unity; for the Greeks, on the contrary, it has been *tritheism*, i.e., excessive insistence on distinction. The call to unity for the two "sister" churches arises from the very profundity of the mystery that we both venerate. In a fully achieved unity, each church would confirm and make the other whole, preserving both from the risk to which each is exposed.

3. Everyone Wants Unity

The problem of unity in diversity is an issue not only in the relationships between various churches; it occurs, in a different way, within each church, in relationship to its various components. Unity is built by means of concentric circles. If the first circle—community, family, and other groupings—is bypassed, what gets spread is not unity, but division.

When rightly ordered, charity, they say, *incipit a seipso*, begins at home. Similarly, unity, if rightly ordered, begins at home—literally, "with oneself," the individual person. We are divided within ourselves. If Jesus were to ask me, as he did the possessed man in the gospel, "What is your name?" I would have to answer truthfully, "My name is Legion; for we are many" (see Mark 5:9). Interior unity or integration of a human being is one of the hardest goals to achieve; growth in inner unity corresponds to growth in holiness.

In a meditation like this, we need to put the spotlight precisely on this specific point, on the unity among us. Let us follow the pattern set by St. Sergius of Radonezh of "overcoming the hateful divisions of this world by contemplating the Trinity," and, we could add, "of the church."

Everyone wants unity. After the word "happiness," there is no other word that speaks as much to the impelling need of the human heart as the word "unity." We are "finite beings, capable of infinity," and that means that we are limited creatures who aspire to go beyond our limitations, to be "in some way everything," *quodammodo omnia,* as they say in philosophy. We do not resign ourselves to being only what we are. Who does not remember in youth a moment of aching need for unity, a desire for the universe to be enclosed in one single spot with everyone gathered together, because you were suffering a sense of separation and loneliness in the world? St. Thomas Aquinas helps explain this: "*One [unum]* is a principle, just as *good [bonum]* is. Hence everything naturally desires unity, just as it desires goodness: and therefore, just as love or desire for good is a cause of sorrow, so also is the love or craving for unity."[5]

All human beings want unity and desire it from the bottom of their hearts. The need for unity is a hunger for the fullness of being. There is a need for unity at the heart not only of marriage, in which two people unite themselves to become one flesh, but also, in a different way, at the heart of the quest for material goods and new knowledge.

Why, then, is it so difficult to achieve unity, if everyone desires it so much? It is because we want unity, of course, but . . . unity around *our* point of view. Our view seems so obvious, so reasonable, that we are astounded that others do not agree and instead insist on *their* point of view. We even carefully lay out the path for others to come where we are and join us. The problem is that the person in front of me is doing exactly the same thing to me. No unity will ever be achieved if we go about it this way; unity takes the opposite path.

4. The Trinity Teaches Us the Path to Unity

The Trinity shows us the true path to unity. The Eastern fathers, proceeding from the divine *Persons,* rather than from the concept of *nature,* found themselves needing to affirm the divine unity in another way. They did that by developing the doctrine of *perichoresis,* literally, "interpenetration or dependence of persons or natures." (The Latin fathers subsequently adopted this concept, calling it *circumincessio,* but it came from the Orthodox.) Applied to the Trinity, *perichoresis* expresses the union of the three Persons in their one essence.[6] It means that the three Persons are united, but without being confused or intermingled; each Person "identifies" with the other, gives himself to the other, and sustains the existence of the other. According to a more modern interpretation, the *perichoresis* is "the unity of activity within the Three toward one another."[7]

This concept comes from Christ's words: "Believe me that I am in the Father and the Father in me" (John 14:11). Jesus has extended this principle to his relationship to us: "I am in my Father, and you in me, and I in you" (14:20); "I in them and thou in me, that they may become perfectly one" (17:23).

The divine *perichoresis* is the path to true unity that we should follow in the church. St. Paul indicates its foundation when he says that we are "individually members one of another" (Romans 12:5). The *perichoresis* in God is based on the unity of nature, and in us on the fact that we are "one body and one spirit" (see 1 Corinthians 12:12-13).

The apostle helps us understand what it means for us in practice to live the *perichoresis,* or mutual interdependence: "If one member suffers, all suffer together; if one member is honored, all rejoice together" (1 Corinthians 12:26); "Bear one another's burdens, and so fulfil the law of Christ" (Galatians 6:2). The "burdens" of others are sicknesses, limitations, anxieties, and even defects and sins. Living out the *perichoresis* means "identifying ourselves" with others, to walk, as we say, in their shoes, to seek first to understand rather than to judge.

In the Trinity, every Person speaks well of the others, and this reminds us of the exhortation from St. James, "Do not speak evil against one another, brethren" (4:11). There is only one "place" in the world where the rule of "love your neighbor as yourself" is perfectly put into practice, and that is the Trinity! Every divine Person loves the others as himself.

Let us look at how the principle of rejoicing in the honor of others shines forth in the Trinity. The three divine Persons are always engaged in glorifying each other. The Father glorifies the Son; the Son glorifies the Father (see John 17:4); the Paraclete will glorify the Son (see 16:14). Each one devotes himself to making the others known. The Son teaches us to cry *"Abba!"*; the Spirit teaches us to cry "Jesus is Lord!" and "Come, Lord," *Maranatha*. Each of them teaches us to speak not his own name but the name of the two other Persons.

How different the atmosphere is when we try to live out these sublime ideals in any social setting! Taking this approach, a person could rejoice at someone's nomination for a certain post of honor (for example, in being named a cardinal) as if he himself had been nominated. But let us have the saints tell us these things; they alone have the right to do so since they put it into practice:

If you love unity, whoever in it has anything has it also for you. Take away envy, and what I have is yours; let me take away envy, and what you have is mine. Jealousy separates, right reason joins. . . . Again, in the body, only the hand works; but does it work only for itself? It also worked for the eye; for if some blow were coming and not going against the hand but only against the face, does the hand say, "I do not move myself because it is not aiming at me"?[8]

In the same way, whoever has a charism or exercises a ministry in the church does not do so for his or her sake but for the sake of all.

Contemplating the Trinity truly does assist us in "overcoming hateful divisions." The first miracle the Spirit performed at Pentecost was to make the disciples "of one heart and soul" (Acts 4:32). He is always ready to repeat that miracle and to transform *dis-cord* into *con-cord* every time. We can be divided in what we think—on doctrinal or pastoral questions that are legitimately debated in the church—but we should never be divided in heart: *In dubiis libertas, in omnibus vero caritas* ("liberty in doubtful things, charity in all things"). This means precisely to imitate the unity of the Trinity, that is, "unity in diversity."

5. Entering into the Trinity

There is something that is more blessed that we can do with regard to the Trinity than contemplate and imitate it: we can enter into it! We cannot wrap our arms around the ocean, but we can enter into it. We cannot encompass the mystery of the Trinity with our minds, but we can enter into it!

Christ has left us a concrete way to do that: the Eucharist. In Rublëv's icon, the three angels are positioned around a table; there is a cup on that table and, inside the cup, a lamb. There is no simpler or more effective way to tell us that the Trinity meets us every day in the Eucharist. The banquet of Abraham at the oaks of Mamre is a figure of that banquet. The visitation to Abraham by the Three is renewed for us each time we receive Communion.

The doctrine of the trinitarian *perichoresis* is also enlightening here. It tells us that wherever one Person of the Trinity is, the other two are also present, inseparably united. Communion actualizes the words of Christ in a strict sense: "I in them and you in me" (John 17:23); "He who has seen me has seen the Father" (John 14:9). St. Cyril of Alexandria, in his typical theological rigor, has formulated this truth that inextricably links the Trinity to the Eucharist: "We are completed in our unity with God the Father through Christ. By receiving into ourselves bodily and spiritually what the Son is by nature, we become participants and partners of all the supreme nature."[9]

We will never be able to appreciate enough the grace that is offered to us in the Eucharist. Table companions of the Trinity!

6. Can We Dispense with the Trinity?

What I have said is enough to make us understand how mistaken Immanuel Kant is when he asserts, "The doctrine of the Trinity, taken literally, has *no practical relevance at all*,"[10] meaning that it is irrelevant to people's lives and the Christian life. On the contrary, it is the one thing that is relevant!

The trinitarian mystery is the only answer to modern atheism. If the idea of a one and triune God (rather than a vague

"Supreme Being") were vibrantly alive in theology, it would not have been so easy for some people to believe Ludwig Feuerbach's theory that God is a merely a projection of humanity shaped according to its essence. What need do people have to separate themselves into three—Father, Son, and Holy Spirit? Feuerbach's theory demolishes vague deism, but not faith in the triune God.

Some people today might want to put parentheses around the dogma of the Trinity to facilitate dialogue with the other great monotheistic religions.[11] That would be a suicidal move. It would be like removing a person's backbone in order to make him walk more quickly. The Trinity has so profoundly marked theology, liturgy, spirituality, and the whole of Christian life that to renounce it would mean starting a new religion that is completely different.

What needs to happen instead is to move this mystery out of theology books and into our lives. All the great theologians today seem convinced that everything in Christianity stands or falls with the doctrine of the Trinity, and they are committed to bringing that doctrine back to the center of attention—for example, Karl Barth, Karl Rahner, Hans Urs von Balthasar, and others.

What is still needed, though, is making this new focus available to everyone in such a way that the mystery is not only studied and correctly formulated, but lived, adored, and enjoyed. Baptized Christians must learn to *live with* the Trinity. They are the three Persons who are the most intimate for us—closer than a husband, a wife, a father, a mother—because "they make their home with us" (see John 14:23).

The Christian life unfolds from beginning to end under the

sign and in the presence of the Trinity. At birth we were baptized "in the name of the Father, Son, and Holy Spirit." And at the end, if we have the grace to die a Christian death, we will hear at our bedside, "Go from this world, Christian soul, in the name of the Father who created you, of the Son who redeemed you, and of the Holy Spirit who sanctified you." Between birth and death there are other times, so-called "passages," that for a Christian are all marked by an invocation to the Trinity. In the name of the Father, Son, and Holy Spirit, men and women are joined in matrimony and exchange rings, and priests and bishops are ordained. Contracts, court judgments, and every important act of civil and religious life were once done in the name of the Trinity.

The Trinity is the *womb* in which we were conceived (see Ephesians 1:4), and it also the port toward which we navigate. It is the "ocean of peace" from which everything flows out and to which everything flows back. It is the house in which there are "many rooms."

Let us close by making ours the sentiments of that great cantor of the Trinity in the Eastern Church, St. Gregory Nazianzus, as he concludes the long poem about his life:

I shall be all withdrawn in God. Let tongues prattle on about me like empty winds. I've had more than enough of that, people often assailed me with slanders and often with extravagant praise. I seek to live somewhere that is free from evil people, somewhere where I can turn to heavenly pursuits with my spirit alone. To the churches I shall bestow my tears. Through all the vicissitudes of my life

God has led me to this point. Tell me, Logos of Father, whither now? Towards the unshaken seat, I pray, where is my Trinity, and that united brightness by the faint reflections of which we are now upraised.[12]

1. This was the motto of the fourteenth-century Russian monk, St. Sergius of Radonezh; see Nicholas Zernov, *The Russians and Their Church*, 3rd ed. (Crestwood, NY: St. Vladimir's Seminary Press, 1994), p. 41.

2. Paul Evdokimov, *The Art of the Icon: A Theology of Beauty*, trans. by Fr. Steven Bigham (Redondo Beach CA: Oakwood Publications, 1990), p. 248.

3. Gregory of Nazianzus, "Concerning His Own Affairs," lines 195–202, in *Saint Gregory Nazianzus: Three Poems*, trans. by Denis Molaise Mechan, OSB, vol. 75 of *The Fathers of the Church* (Washington, DC: The Catholic University of America Press, 1987), p. 33.

4. Théodore de Regnon, *Études de théologie positive sur la Sainte Trinité* [*Studies in Positive Theology of the Holy Trinity*], vol. 1 (Paris: Victor Retaux, 1892), p. 433.

5. Thomas Aquinas, "Causes of Sorrow or Pain," I–II, q. 36, a. 3, *Summa Theologica*, vol. 2, trans. by Fathers of the English Dominican Province (Westminster, MD: Christian Classics, 1981), p. 749.

6. See Cyril of Alexandria, *De Trinitate*, 23 (PG 77, 1164 B); John of Damascus, *The Orthodox Faith*, 3, 7, trans. by Frederic H. Chase, Jr., vol. 37 in *The Fathers of the Church* (New York: Fathers of the Church, Inc., 1958), pp. 281–84.

8. Augustine, *Tractates on the Gospel of John*, 32, 8, trans. by John W. Rettig, vol. 88 of *The Fathers of the Church* (Washington, DC: The Catholic University of America Press, 1993), p. 48.

9. Cyril of Alexandria, *Commentary on John*, XI, 12 (PG 74), p. 564.

10. Immanuel Kant, *Conflict of the Faculties*, Appendix II, 1, a, trans. and intro. by Mary J. Gregor (Lincoln, NB: University of Nebraska Press, 1979), p. 65.

11. Hans Küng, *On Being a Christian*, trans. by Edward Quinn (Garden City, NY: Doubleday & Co., 1976): "The Christological element is the specific feature [of Christianity]" (p. 474), but "the triple divinity . . . [is] anything but specifically Christian" (p. 473); "We can no longer accept the mythical ideas of that [New Testament] age about a being descended from God, existing before time and beyond this world in a heavenly state; a 'story of gods,' in which two (or even three) divine beings were involved, is not for us" (p. 446); "The monotheistic faith taken over from Israel and held in common with Islam must never be abandoned in any doctrine of the Trinity. There is no God but God" (p. 476).

12. St. Gregory of Nazianzus, "Concerning His Own Life," lines 1935–49, in *Saint Gregory Nazianzus: Three Poems*, trans. by Denis Molaise Meehan, OSB, vol. 75 of *The Fathers of the Church* (Washington, DC: The Catholic University of America Press, 1987), p. 130.

Chapter 2

Contemplating the Trinity to Overcome the Great Unhappiness of the World:
THE TRINITY IN WESTERN SPIRITUALITY

Blessed Angela of Foligno was trying once to make her confessor, Brother Arnaldo, understand how impossible it was for her to try to express her mystical experience in words because, she said, the more we know God, the less we can speak about him. Her confessor was still not satisfied and urged her to explain herself more clearly. Finally she said, "Would that when you go to preach you could understand, as I understand. . . . For then you would be absolutely unable to say anything about God . . . and thus if you had attained this state, you would then say to the people . . . 'Go with God, because about God I can say nothing.'"[1] And then he would leave the pulpit in silence.

At the beginning of this second meditation on the Trinity, I wonder if I would not do better to use the words of Blessed Angela and also say, "Brothers, go with God's blessing; I am not in a position to tell you anything about God." Unable to add anything on my own, I will seek help this time in what the church has experienced of God and of the Trinity. In this instance, I will rely on the rich doctrine and experience of the Latin Church.

1. The *Trinity* by Masaccio

I will begin here as I did in the first chapter, with one of the most traditional artistic representations of the Trinity, to try to sum up the spirit of this tradition. In art textbooks, the title *Trinity* refers to a very specific artistic subject present from the Middle Ages on throughout the West: God the Father, with wide-open arms supporting the cross of the Son, while the dove of the Holy Spirit hovers between their faces. In the Byzantine world, the Trinity is represented by three angels around a table, but in the Latin world by three divine Persons at Calvary. There are innumerable representations of this kind, from the simplest and most popular to the greatest masterpieces. I once counted seven such examples in one single room of a museum in Florence. The most famous is Masaccio's *Trinity*, a fresco in the church of Santa Maria Novella in Florence that represents a milestone in the history of Western painting because it inaugurated the new technique of perspective. In the Kunsthistorisches Museum in Vienna there is a large canvas by Albrecht Dürer depicting the same subject.

The Western representation, therefore, does not try to depict the Trinity as it is in heaven or in speculative theology, but as it has revealed itself in the history of salvation. Not being able to represent the immaterial and the invisible, artists had an advantage over the theologians. They did not have to wait for Karl Rahner, to know that "The Trinity of the economy of salvation *is* the immanent Trinity and vice versa,"[2] and that all we can say about the Trinity has to begin with what has been revealed to us in salvation history.

2. The Trinity and the Cross

This mode of representing the Trinity was itself a precursor and merits our attention today for that reason: it anticipated centuries ago the theme of the suffering of God that has most recently characterized trinitarian doctrine in the West, both Catholic and Protestant. I refer to the positions of two of the most qualified representatives of this theology, Jürgen Moltmann (Protestant) and Hans Urs von Balthasar (Catholic).

According to Moltmann, the Trinity was revealed at the cross, and we can perceive it there: ". . . the theology of the cross must be the doctrine of the Trinity and the doctrine of the Trinity must be the theology of the cross. . . ."[3] In the act of "delivering up" his Son to the cross for us, God makes himself known as Father:

> In the forsakenness of the Son the Father also forsakes himself. . . . Jesus suffers dying in forsakenness, but not death itself; for men can no longer "suffer" death because suffering presupposes life. But the Father who abandons him and delivers him up suffers the death of the Son in the infinite grief of love. . . . To understand what happened between Jesus and his God and Father on the cross, it is necessary to talk in trinitarian terms.[4]

Von Balthasar starts from the same premises, but he goes further. For him what happens at the cross is, in some way, a reflection of what happens within the Trinity itself since before time began. In his act of generating the Son, the Father dispossesses himself totally of his divinity to give it to the Son, in an absolute renunciation of being God by himself. It is a "theo-drama," a divine drama that unfolds within the bosom of God himself; the infinite movement of the divine Persons giving themselves to one another implies a movement of separation, with the two entities maintained and transcended thanks to the Spirit.[5] The Holy Spirit, who is the love of God in a Person, is, consequently, also "the sorrow of God in a Person" and is thus present at the cross.[6]

These new developments in trinitarian theology had a historical impetus. People wondered, How do we still speak of God after Auschwitz? Where was God then? The answer that was given from a rereading of the Bible and from certain voices buried in tradition was that God is with people in their suffering. God is not unfeeling; in a mysterious way he suffers for human beings and with them: "God the Father suffers the suffering of love."[7]

The International Theological Commission pronounced a substantially positive judgment on this new direction,[8] and, with all the required clarifications and cautions, it was favorably received by John Paul II in his encyclical *Dominum et vivificantem*. I was able to recognize in my own preaching ministry the extraordinary fruit that this proclamation brought forth in people: it touched people, it helped overcome seemingly unanswerable objections, and it gave new significance to the affirmation that God is Father.

Recently, however, I have become convinced that something was left out, and that to continue to present it without a strong corrective can be risky.[9] On a pastoral level, it is not enough to respond to human suffering by proclaiming that God suffers too. People do not want God only as a companion in their suffering, they are looking to him as the guarantor of joy itself. Otherwise, there is the danger of falling back into the ancient pagan tragic belief that there is a power stronger than God himself, to which he is also subject, the *anankē*, harsh Necessity and Fate. Augustine wrote, "When I seek you, my God, what I am seeking is a life of happiness,"[10] and that is true for everyone.

The weakness in the doctrine of trinitarian suffering in certain authors is that it is based on the "crucified God" and does not adequately take into account the resurrection, that is, the victory already accomplished over suffering and death. According to them, the resurrection of Christ would not have any real intersection point with life in the present-day world. It would only serve to guarantee to us that in the end there will be a redemption and a reversal in the eschatological fulfillment, when the Son will definitively hand over the kingdom to the Father—in other words, when all the redeemed rise from the dead.[11] It is only the long shadow of the cross—not yet illuminated by the light of the resurrection (except in an anticipatory way as a promise)—that stretches out over our present life.

3. Trinitarian Joy

It is clear, then, that what is missing in the theology of God's suffering is the proclamation of God's joy. The Latin tradition possesses within itself the remedy and the necessary corrective for a trinitarian doctrine that risks becoming "gloomy" when it speaks too unilaterally of separation, abandonment, and forsakenness among the divine Persons. The Latin tradition has always left wide room for the theme of *gaudium Trinitatis* ("trinitarian joy"), with the Holy Spirit as the personification of that joy.

St. Hilary of Poitiers tells us that the Father is infinity; the Son, the manifestation; and the Holy Spirit, the enjoyment (*fruito*).[12] St. Augustine developed this insight:

> [T]hat inexpressible embrace . . . of the Father and the image is not without enjoyment, without charity, without happiness. So this love, delight, felicity or blessedness (if any human word can be found that is good enough to express it) . . . is the Holy Spirit in the triad, not begotten, but the sweetness of begetter and begotten pervading all creatures according to their capacity with its vast generosity and fruitfulness, that they might all keep their right order and rest in their right places.[13]

In the light of this text, all the sweetness and the joy that exists on the face of the earth appears as a kind of pale reflection of the trinitarian embrace.

Subsequent authors did not hesitate to speak of intratrinitarian life with fervent images of intimacy and of kisses, images that most powerfully evoke communion, enjoyment, and joy. "Surely if the Father kisses and the Son receives the kiss, it is appropriate to think of the Holy Spirit as the kiss."[14]

It is not a question of renouncing either of these two solid achievements of Latin theology—the ancient understanding of God's joy or the modern one about God's suffering—but of holding them together, according to the Catholic approach of "both . . . and" rather than "either . . . or." It is possible to do this. The mystics often speak of a secret joy in some remote part of the soul, even in the midst of darkest times and worst torments, a joy they would not trade for any pleasure in the world whatsoever. Paul himself asserted, "With all our afflictions, I am overjoyed" (2 Corinthians 7:4).

Joy and sorrow are intermingled on many occasions in life, in particular in a woman at the moment of childbirth (see John 16:21). They are not simply juxtaposed, one next to each other, but they are within one another. There is a joy that comes precisely from sorrow, from suffering for a loved one—the joy of sacrifice done out of love. This was the kind of joy Christ had in the depths of his soul on the cross, and this is the kind of joy the Trinity has in its relation to the human beings it has created.

The harmonizing of joy and sorrow is thus through love, to which we always revert when speaking of the Christian God. We read in *The Imitation of Christ* that "there is no living a life of love without sorrow,"[15] and this principle seems to be realized in a supreme way with respect to God, at least as long as the objects of his love, human beings, are exposed to the danger of being lost. *Dominum et vivificantem* ends its paragraph on the suffering of God by saying, "In a word, this inscrutable and undescribable [sic] *fatherly 'pain' will bring about* above all the wonderful economy of redemptive love in Jesus Christ, so that through the *mysterium pietatis* ["mystery of piety"] love can reveal itself in the history of man as stronger than sin. So that the 'gift' may prevail!"[16]

4. Everyone Wants to Be Happy

It is time to shout to the world that the Trinity is first and foremost joy and happiness. The Trinity is "our resting place," "the flood of delight" in whom our thirst will one day be quenched. St. Sergius of Radonezh said that contemplating the Trinity could "overcome the hateful divisions of this world," but we could also say that "contemplating the Trinity can overcome the great unhappiness of the world."

God is happy! Augustine says that God is happy and makes people happy.[17] Happiness is part of the very mystery of his being. Being the highest good, he is also the highest and infinite happiness. St. Francis of Assisi exclaims, "You are joy; You are . . . joy" in his "Praises of God."[18]

God is happiness for the very same reason that the Trinity is happy: because he is love. Happiness, in fact, is to love and be loved. God, from all eternity, loves his Son with an infinite love, and the Son returns that love with an equally infinite love. The Father finds "all his pleasure," that is, his happiness, in him. Since God is happy, he does everything that he does with joy: he creates with joy (see Job 38:7), he saves with joy, and—as we have seen—he even suffers with joy.

The Holy Spirit, pouring the love of God into hearts (see Romans 5:5), at the same time pours into them the happiness of God that is inseparable from this love. Because of that, one of the first fruits that is produced in our souls is joy (see Galatians 5:22). The happiness of God is like an overflowing river "whose streams make glad the city of God" (Psalm 46:4), i.e., the church.

"We all want to be happy": *Beati omnes esse volumus.* This is the great affirmation in Cicero's *Hortensius* that made such a deep impression on a young Augustine and convinced him, contrary to his skepticism, that there is a commonly held certitude on which to base the search for truth.[19] Just hearing the word "happiness," people perk up, so to speak, and look to see if, by chance, you are able to offer something for their thirst. This is the one thing that unites all people, without exception, whether they are good or evil. No one, in fact, would be evil if he or she did not hope to be happy through that evil thing. Happiness, Dante said, is "That sweet fruit which the care of mortals goes to seek on so many boughs."[20]

We carry the desire to be happy engraved on our hearts, because God has created us in "his image and likeness," and since he is perfect happiness, he made us for happiness too.

But then, we ask ourselves, why are so few people truly happy? And even those who are, why are they happy for such a short time? It is not difficult to discover where the error lies. Scripture tells us, "God is love" (1 John 4:8); people have believed they can reverse the statement and say, "love is God"![21] Revelation tells us that God is happiness; again people invert the order and say, "Happiness is God"! But what happens when we do this? Human beings do not know happiness that is pure, absolute, eternal, and transcendent, just as they do not know absolute love. They know fragments of happiness, which are often reduced to temporary intoxications of the senses, joys that are like fragile glass that always risks being shattered into fragments from one moment to another. In this way people deify the experience of joy and make it an idol. This is, to some extent, the joy sung by Friedrich Schiller in the famous musical ode by Beethoven that was proposed as the official hymn for the European Union: "Joy, beautiful spark of the gods, daughter of Elysium / . . . / All men become brothers where your gentle wing rests. / . . . / All creatures partake of joy at Nature's breast."[22]

This explains why whoever seeks God always finds joy, while the person who seeks joy does not always find God, but often finds only a "dry wet-nurse," ". . . broken cisterns that can hold no water" (Jeremiah 2:13). Augustine says, "you have made us and drawn us to yourself" (*Fecesti nos, Domine, ad te*).[23] It is the whole Trinity that has made us; the Trinity is the Creator-God of Christians. We have been made for the Trinity, and our hearts will be restless until they rest in it. The real hymn to joy is Mary's Magnificat: "My spirit *rejoices* in God" (Luke 1:47).

It is time, I was saying, to begin boldly to proclaim this "joyful message" that God is happiness, and that happiness—not suffering, deprivation, or the cross—will have the last word. St. Paul extended an invitation to the Christians at Philippi to rejoice that sets the tone for the whole third week of Advent: "Rejoice in the Lord always; again I say rejoice." He also explains how a person is to testify to that joy and make it credible: "Let all men know your forbearance . . ." (Philippians 4:5). The word "forbearance" is a translation of the Greek work *epieikēs*, which refers to a set of attitudes that include mercy, forgiveness, and an ability to yield and not to be stubborn. (It is the same vocabulary word from which the word *epicheia* ["equity"] comes, which is used in law.) Christians testify to joy when, avoiding all bitterness and useless resentment in communication with the world and among themselves, they radiate trust and hope.

Whoever is happy is not bitter, is not harsh, and does not feel the need to nitpick everything all the time. People like this know how to keep things in perspective, because they know something that is so much greater; they love because they know they are loved. Paul VI, in his apostolic exhortation on joy written on May 9, 1975, near the end of his pontificate, speaks of a "positive outlook on people and things, the fruit of an enlightened human spirit and fruit of the Holy Spirit. . . ."[24]

5. The Place to Encounter the Trinity

The Latin tradition recognizes a place where we can encounter the Trinity and acquire the power to witness to joy: within our souls. The doctrine of indwelling is also known of course by the Eastern theologians, but in that tradition it is mostly related to the Person of the Holy Spirit. It is Latin theology that developed the full potential of the biblical doctrine of the indwelling of the whole Trinity in our souls: "My Father will love him, and we will come to him and make our home with him" (John 14:23).[25] Pius XII made a place for it in his *Mystici corporis,* saying that, thanks to the Trinity, we are able "to rejoice with a happiness like to that with which the holy and undivided Trinity is happy."[26]

But above all, the doctrine of indwelling can be seen in the lived experience of mystics in the Latin Church. The German Rhenish mystics speak of the "depth of the human soul" as the place where the trinitarian activity is mystically renewed: the Father generates the Son, and together they breathe forth the Holy Spirit. The same conviction, freed from debatable presuppositions, is found in St. John of the Cross. For him, the love spoken of in Romans 5:5—"God's love has been poured into our hearts through the Holy Spirit which has been given to us"—is none other than the love with which the Father eternally loves the Son. It is an overflow of the Trinity's divine love to us. God "raises the soul most sublimely, and informs her that she may breathe in God the same breath of love that the Father breathes in the Son. . . . God grants her the favour of attaining to being deiform and united in the Most Holy Trinity, wherein she becomes God by participation."[27]

Allow me to cite in this regard the testimony of a woman who describes the grace she received during nocturnal prayer:

The Spirit introduced me to the mystery of trinitarian love. The ecstatic exchange of giving and receiving was taking place within me: from Christ, to whom I was united, toward the Father and the Father toward the Son. How can I express the inexpressible? I was not seeing anything but I experienced far more than seeing, and my words are wholly inadequate to describe this reciprocal exchange of joy that was going forth, receiving, and giving. And an intense life flowed from One to Another in that exchange, like warm milk that flows from a mother's breast to the baby's mouth attached to that comfort. And I was that baby, and all of creation participates in the life, the reign, and the glory that was being regenerated by Christ. O holy and living Trinity! I felt as though I were outside of myself for two or three days, and still today this experience remains strongly impressed upon me.

With experiences like these, we can understand St. Thomas Aquinas's affirmation that "grace is nothing else than a beginning of glory in us."[28] The true "breasts" from which creatures can "nourish themselves with joy" are now revealed.

From the Latin vision of the Trinity, especially from the doctrine of indwelling, we hear a call: *In teipsum redi, in interiorem hominem habitat veritas:* enter into yourself, for it is within the interior of a person that truth, the Trinity, dwells! We should seek to imitate Blessed Elizabeth of the Trinity, whose spiritual discipline consisted of "burying myself, so to speak, in the depths of my soul to lose myself in the Trinity who dwells in it."[29]

6. The Trinity at Christ's Nativity

I spoke of the joy of the Trinity to be rediscovered in our day. I should say that Western artists anticipated the theologians in this case, as well. Besides the theme of the Trinity at the cross, another theme in paintings is the Trinity at Christ's birth. It shows the Father gazing ecstatically at the Child in the manger, with his arms outstretched—this time in a gesture of pleasure and joy—and between the Father and the Son, here as well, the Holy Spirit in the form of a dove. Filippo Lippi, a Carmelite brother, has left us a famous example of this in a painting that is now in the Berlin Museum. This is the same subject depicted by Andrea della Robbia in his famous terracotta of the nativity housed in the shrine at La Verna in Tuscany.

What is the reason for the Father's joy at Christmas? Duns Scotus would reply, "God is happy because finally there is someone outside himself *by whom he is loved* in the supreme way that he deserves: the Incarnate Word."[30] But if it is true that "it is more blessed to give than to receive" (Acts 20:35), to give love than to receive it, perhaps we should be more precise: God the Father is happy because finally there is someone outside of himself *whom he can love* in a supreme way that is worthy of him. He has Jesus Christ and, with him, all of us who have become sons in the Son. "The first-born of all creation," through whom and for whom "all things were created" (Colossians 1: 15, 16), has appeared on earth. God sees that finally "everything is very good" (see Genesis 1:31) and rejoices as he did at the beginning of creation.

This image calls to mind the words of the English mystic Julian of Norwich, "And then I saw that God rejoices that he is our Father: and God rejoices that he is our Mother: and God rejoices that he is our true Spouse, and our soul his beloved wife."[31] God is happy and content: this is the affirmation we needed to hear about the one and triune God at the beginning of the new millennium.

Let us conclude with the trinitarian doxology that completes the eucharistic prayer at Mass: "Through him, with him, and in him, in the unity of the Holy Spirit, all glory and honor is yours, almighty Father, forever and ever. Amen."

1. Blessed Angela of Foligno, *Memorial*, VII, in *Angela of Foligno: Complete Works*, pref. by Romana Guarnieri, trans. by Paul Lachance, OFM (New York: Paulist Press, 1934), p. 192.

2. Karl Rahner, "Remarks on the Treatise 'De Trinitate,'" in *A Rahner Reader*, ed. by Gerald A. McCool (New York: Seabury Press, 1975), p. 139.

3. Jürgen Moltmann, *The Crucified God: The Cross of Christ as the Foundation and Criticism of Christian Theology*, trans. by R. A. Wilson and John Bowden (New York: Harper & Row, 1973), p. 241.

4. Moltmann, p. 243.

5. See Hans Urs von Balthasar, *Theo-Drama: Theological Dramatic Theory*, trans. by Graham Harrison (San Francisco: Ignatius Press, 1988).

6. See Heribert Mühlen, *Theologie und Glaube* [*Theology and*

Faith] (Paderborn, Germany: Verlag F. Schöningh, 1988).

7. Origen, "Homily on Ezekiel," 6, 6 (GSC 1925), p. 384.

8. See the document "Teologia, cristologia, antropologia" ["Theology, Christology, Anthropology"], in *Civiltà Cattolica* 34 (1983), pp. 50–65.

9. See Bertran de Margerie, "Trinité," in *Catholicisme* XV (1962), pp. 333–53.

10. Augustine, *Confessions*, X, 20, vol. 1, trans. by Maria Boulding, OSB, in *The Works of St. Augustine*, ed. John E. Rotelle, OSA (Hyde Park, NY: New City Press, 1997), p. 256.

11. See Moltmann, p. 162ff.

12. See Hilary of Poitiers, *The Trinity*, II, 1, trans. by Stephen McKenna, CSSR, vol. 25 in *The Fathers of the Church* (New York: Fathers of the Church, Inc., 1954), p. 36.

13. Augustine, *The Trinity*, VI, 2, 11, trans. by Edmund Hill, OP, vol. 5 of *The Works of St. Augustine*, ed. by John E. Rotelle, OSA (Brooklyn, NY: New City Press, 1991), p. 213.

14. Bernard of Clairvaux, *Sermons on the Song of Songs*, 8, 1, in *Bernard of Clairvaux: Selected Works*, intro. by Jean Leclercq, OSB, trans. and foreword by G. R. Evans (New York: Paulist Press, 1987), p. 237; see Isaac of Stella, *Discourses* 45, 12 (SCh 339), p. 104; see Aelred of Rievaulx, *The Mirror of Charity*, I, 20, 57, trans. by Adrian Walker (London: A. R. Mowbray & Co., 1962), pp. 30–31.

15. Thomas à Kempis, *The Imitation of Christ*, III, 5, 8, trans. by Ronald Knox and Michael Oakley (South Bend, IN: Greenlawn Press, 1990), p. 90.

16. Pope John Paul II, *Dominum et vivificantem* [The Holy Spirit in the Life of the Church and the World], 39 (Boston: St. Paul Books and Media, 1986), p. 63.

17. See Augustine, *The City of God*, IX, 15, trans. by John Healey (New York: E. P. Dutton & Sons, 1945), p. 266.

18. Francis of Assisi, "Praises of God," in *Francis and Clare: The Complete Works*, pref. by John Vaughn, OFM, trans. by Regis J. Armstrong, OFM Cap, and Ignatius C. Brady, OFM (New York: Paulist Press, 1982), p. 100.

19. See Augustine, *The Trinity*, XIII, 2, 7, p. 348.

20. Dante Alighieri, *Purgatorio*, XXVII, 115–16, vol. 2 in *The Divine Comedy*, trans and com. by John D. Sinclair (New York: Oxford University Press, 1939), p. 357.

21. See Ludwig Feuerbach, *The Essence of Christianity*, foreword by H. Richard Niehbuhr, intro. by Karl Barth, trans. by George Eliot (New York: Harper Torchbooks, 1957), p. 264.

22. "An die Freude," Appendix I, in Nicholas Cook, *Beethoven: Symphony No. 9* (Cambridge: Cambridge University Press, 1993), p. 109.

23. Augustine, *Confessions*, I, 1, p. 39.

24. Pope Paul VI, *Gaudete in domino* [On Christian Joy], Conclusion, in *The Teachings of Pope Paul VI*, vol. 8 (Vatican City: Libreria Editrice Vaticana, 1975), p. 504.

25. See Roberto Moretti and Guy-M. Bertrand, "Inhabitation," in *Dictionnaire de spiritualité ascétique et mystique, doctrine et histoire* [*Dictionary of Ascetic and Mystical Spirituality, Doctrine an d History*], ed. by Marcel Viller, SJ, et al., vol. 7b (Paris: Beauchesne, 1971), col. 1735–67.

26. Pope Pius XII, *Mystici corporis* [On the Mystical Body of Christ], 80, in *The Papal Encyclicals, 1939–1958*, ed. by Claudia Carlen (Wilmington, NC: McGrath Publishing, 1981), p. 53.

27. John of the Cross, *Spiritual Canticle [A]* stanza 38, 2–3, in *The Complete Works of Saint John of the Cross*, vol. 2, trans. and

ed. by E. Allison Peers (Westminster, MD: Newman Press, 1949), p. 176.

28. St. Thomas Aquinas, *Summa Theologica*, "Whether Charity Is Infused according to the Capacity of Our Natural Gifts," II–II, q. 24, a.3, reply obj. 2, vol. 3, trans. by Fathers of the English Dominican Province (Westminster, MD: Christian Classics, 1981), p. 1271.

29. Elizabeth of the Trinity, "Letter 185," in *I Have Found God: Complete Works, Elizabeth of the Trinity* , vol. 2, trans. by Anne Englund Nash (Washington DC: ICS Publications, 1995), p. 136.

30. John Duns Scotus, *Opus Parisiense* III, 7, 4, (*Opera omnia*, XXIII, [Paris: Apud L. Vivès, 1894), p. 303.

31. Julian of Norwich, *The Revelations of Divine Love*, 52, trans. by James Welsh, SJ (St. Meinrad's, IN: Abbey Press, 1975), p. 144.

Chapter 3

In the Father, through the Son, in the Holy Spirit: THE TRINITARIAN DYNAMICS OF PRAYER

1. Pray and Do What You Will

In his apostolic letter *Novo millennio ineunte,* John Paul II says that as the church enters the third millennium, holiness "is the foundation of the pastoral planning in which we are involved."[1] I would like to welcome that summons and reflect on certain aspects of Christian holiness in the context of the trinitarian mystery. In that same letter, the pope speaks of "a high standard of ordinary Christian living,"[2] and I believe that high standard is ultimately none other than the most holy Trinity.

In this meditation let us reflect on prayer, which is the presupposition and indispensable means of all progress on the path of holiness. "This training in holiness," the pope continues, "calls for a Christian life distinguished above all *in the art of prayer.* . . . But we well know that prayer cannot be taken for granted. We have to learn to pray, as though learning this art ever anew from the lips of the Divine Master himself, like the first disciples: 'Lord, teach us to pray!' (Luke 11:1)."[3]

The fact that prayer is, as the Scripture says, "of value in every way" (1 Timothy 4:8), that it is necessary in all aspects of the spiritual life, has been confirmed many times by the saints. Blessed Angela of Foligno says,

Therefore if you want to begin and to receive this divine light, pray. If you have begun to make progress and want this life intensified within you, pray. And if you have reached the summit of perfection, and want to be superillumined so as to remain in that state, pray.

If you want faith, pray. If you want hope, pray. If you want charity, pray. If you want poverty, pray. If you want obedience, pray. If you want chastity, pray. If you want humility, pray. If you want meekness, pray. If you want fortitude, pray. If you want some virtue, pray. . . . The more you are tempted, the more you should persevere in prayer. And by the very fact that you persevere in your prayers, you put yourself in a position to be tempted. . . . But by the very perseverance in your prayers you will be freed from temptations. Finally, it is through prayer that you will be enlightened, liberated, cleansed, and united with God.[4]

Augustine says, "Love and do what you will";[5] we can also say just as truly, "Pray and do what you will."

2. True Trinitarian Prayer

Building upon this premise, I come to the specific theme of this meditation, trinitarian prayer. The same papal letter goes on to say,

Wrought in the Holy Spirit, this reciprocity opens us, through Christ and in Christ, to contemplation of the Father's face. Learning this *Trinitarian shape of Christian prayer* and living it fully, above all in the liturgy, the summit and source of the Church's life, but also in personal experience, is the secret of a truly vital Christianity, which has no reason to fear the future, because it returns continually to the sources and finds in them new life.[6]

We can first ask the question: what does "trinitarian prayer" mean? What prayer can be called trinitarian in the strictest sense? The incident that led to St. Basil's composition of *On the Holy Spirit*, which he narrates at the beginning of that treatise, can help us with the answer. On one occasion, praying with the people, he sometimes addressed the final doxology "to the Father, together *with* the Son *and* the Holy Spirit," and at other times "to the Father *through* the Son and *in* the Holy Spirit." Some of the people accused him of using peculiar and contradictory expressions. They were sympathizers with the Anomoean heresy that held to the inequality and subordination of the Son and Holy Spirit with respect to the Father. They insisted on the second formula, believing that it expressed the correct doctrine.

St. Basil wrote his treatise to respond to that objection. He used the formula "to the Father, and to the Son, and to the Holy Spirit" precisely because putting all three Persons on the same level in strict coordination affirmed their equality in nature and honor. He was not abandoning the traditional formula for a new one, but merely wishing to clarify the true meaning intended by the church. (This is exactly what the Council of Nicea had done when it introduced the concept of *homoousios*, of one essence, to articulate the true meaning of biblical statements about the Son.)

St. Basil defended the legitimacy of both formulas and used them interchangeably throughout his treatise. The liturgy, whether Eastern or Western, has followed him in this respect. If at times, as in the *Gloria Patri*, we find the formula "Glory be to the Father, and to the Son, and to the Holy Spirit," at other times, in the doxology of the canon, in the prefaces, and at the end of prayers we find instead the original formula, "to the Father, through Christ, and in the unity of the Holy Spirit."

Once we have overcome the risk of a heretical interpretation of subordination, we can without hesitation, then, validate the trinitarian formula "to the Father, through Christ, in the Holy Spirit." It is the most common expression in the New Testament and incorporates the true sense of trinitarian prayer. (The only instance where the alternate formula is used is in Matthew 28:19: ". . . baptizing them in the name of the Father and of the Son and of the Holy Spirit.") Paul speaks constantly of Christian prayer as a prayer addressed to the Father (*Abba*) through Christ, in the Holy Spirit or—and this is the same thing—of a prayer made "in the Spirit of the Son": "Through him [Christ] we both have access *in* the Spirit *to* the Father" [emphasis added] (Ephesians 2:18).

This formula is based on the Trinity as it was revealed to us in salvation history (the economic Trinity) and not on the atemporal Trinity (the immanent Trinity). The Son and Holy Spirit appear, to use St. Irenaeus' image, as the "two hands" through which the Father brought forth the world in creation and drew it back to himself in the redemption.[7]

Why do I say that this is the only case of trinitarian prayer in the strict sense? Because in this case the Trinity is not only the object and terminus of the prayer but also the subject of the prayer. When we say, "Glory be to the Father and to the Son and to the Holy Spirit," we position ourselves on one side with the Trinity on the other. This is not the case when we pray "through Christ, in the unity of the Holy Spirit, all glory and honor are yours, almighty Father." Here we become involved in the very rhythm of trinitarian life in the movement between one Person and another. The Trinity is not, so to speak, at the head of the line but is itself the line along which our prayer passes. This is a prayer made with the Trinity and not just to the Trinity. Because of the love infused in us by the Holy Spirit, we love God though God; we can say the same about prayer in general: "We pray to God through God." Christian prayer is distinct from all other types of prayer precisely because of this.

The expression *per Christum* ("through Christ") is a prepositional phrase indicating not only means and location but also cause. To give thanks to the Father "through Jesus Christ" means to give thanks to him *because of* Christ, for the infinite gift that he is to the world. This is the reason that eternity will not suffice to thank the Father, and that the Father will never tire of being thanked for all eternity.

We should not, however, make this a rigid pattern, as though the Father were always the only fixed terminus of prayer. He is sometimes the source of it and initiates its movement. The ascending pattern of "to the Father, through the Son, and in the Holy Spirit" finds its perfect correlation in Scripture in the descending pattern of "from the Father, through the Son, and in the Holy Spirit." There is also here a perfect circularity and reciprocity among the divine Persons. The Father reveals the Son, speaks of him to us, and exhorts us to listen to him. Paul prays to the Father that the faithful will be strengthened in the Holy Spirit and that Christ will dwell in their hearts (see Ephesians 3:14ff.). At times the Holy Spirit is also the one who initiates the prayer, as when he "helps us in our weakness . . . and intercedes for us . . . according to the will of God" (Romans 8:26-27).

Experience confirms all this. Many people, after receiving the Holy Spirit in a new way and experiencing the famous "new Pentecost," have been led by him to discover trinitarian prayer. At times Jesus speaks to them of the Father, like a brother who exhorts another brother to present himself without fear to the Father of them both, almost pushing him forward gently by the shoulders. At times it is the Father who seems eager to reveal an infinite number of things about the Son to them and to communicate his enthusiasm, his pride, and his joy in him. At times it is the Holy Spirit who teaches them to address the Father as *Abba* and to address the Son, Jesus, as "Lord." There is a sense of new horizons opening up, one after another, that takes one's breath away and leaves one speechless. The Spirit who "searches everything" allows us a glimpse into "the depths of God" (see 1 Corinthians 2:10).

I believe the divine Persons are not offended if we "play on" their "differences" a bit. I will explain with an example. As a preacher, I find myself at times needing to speak about the Son or the Holy Spirit or the Father. I have discovered a trick to get their help. If I need to speak about the Son, I tell the Father that he cannot leave me without the anointing of the Spirit, since Jesus has given me the Holy Spirit so many times to speak about the Father. And I do the same, in turn, with the other Person. I have to say, with complete amazement, that the "trick" works.

We can ally ourselves with the Spirit—and almost ask his complicity—to prepare a celebration for the Father, as children do for their fathers with the help of their mothers. And then we can reverse the alliance and join ourselves with the Father to honor Jesus and the Spirit, and so on. Jesus said, "If you ask anything of the Father, he will give it you in my name" (John 16:23). But this also applies to the other two divine Persons. Whatever we ask Jesus in the name of the Father, he will give it to us; whatever we ask the Spirit in the name of Jesus, he will give it to us.

Oh, how wonderful it is to have the Trinity as our God! When we discover the Trinity, we are no longer tempted to exchange Christian monotheism for any other monotheism. I would feel sorry for any God who had no one with whom to communicate and to share his joy with the profundity that is uniquely his. I think he would feel himself tremendously alone and unhappy! The proof of the Trinity's existence appears on the first page of the Bible: "God created man in his own image," and precisely because we were to be in his image, he added, "It is not good that the man should be alone" (Genesis 1:27; 2:18).

3. Trinitarian Prayer in the Spirit

Trinitarian prayer can take a variety of forms. The highest form is the Mass, not so much because of the continual presence of the trinitarian formulas in the Mass that we have discussed, but because of its fundamental orientation. Everything we receive at Mass comes "from the Father, through the Son, and in the Holy Spirit." The Father so loved the world that he gave his only-begotten Son for its salvation; the Son, Jesus Christ, so loved human beings that he gave his life for them. The Father and Son desire so much to have them united to themselves that they give them their Spirit, their very life. And the Mass is all this!

This descending pattern is particularly visible in the current Eucharist Prayer IV, which closely follows the anaphora of St. Basil:

Father, you so loved the world
that . . . you *sent* your only Son to be our Savior. . . .
He gave *himself up* to death. . . .
He *sent* the Holy Spirit from you, Father,
as his first gift to those who believe.[8]

Conversely, everything that is offered in the Mass—the bread and wine, praise, prayers, ourselves, Christ—is offered to the Father through the Son and in the Holy Spirit, just as the final doxology indicates. Mass can be a "bath" in the Trinity every day, a *full immersion* in its mystery.

The Our Father is also an intrinsically trinitarian prayer in the Spirit, even if it is addressed only to the Father. Whenever a believer calls God "Father," we know that it is through the operation of the Spirit of the Son, who cries *"Abba."*

St. Basil insists on the trinitarian character of Christian worship and contemplation. In his treatise he says that the Holy Spirit is "the place" that we should enter to contemplate and adore God. He applies, in a spiritual sense, to the person who prays, the episode of Moses entering "in a cleft of the rock" in order to contemplate God as he passes by. Basil says that the cleft refers precisely to contemplation in the Holy Spirit (see Exodus 33:22). "Where have we learnt this? From the Lord himself in the words, *'the true worshippers shall worship the Father in Spirit and in truth'* [John 4:23]."[9]

The wonderful thing is that this "cleft in the rock" really exists: it is inside of us, in our own hearts. We can hide ourselves in it even in the middle of a conversation, liturgy, or a sermon. We do that not to escape or absent ourselves, but to make ourselves even more present, present to the Present One.

Certain people clearly have this capacity, and observing them has always edified and motivated me to meditation. It is perhaps the only possible way we have of being, as they say, "contemplatives in action."

Today prayer in the Spirit can also be found in a different form in groups that have emerged here and there in the church who pray various kinds of inspired prayer. Participating in such groups helps us understand what Paul meant when he wrote to the Ephesians, "Be filled with the Spirit, addressing one another in psalms and hymns and spiritual songs, singing and making melody to the Lord with all your heart, always and for everything giving thanks in the name of our Lord Jesus Christ to God the Father" (5:18-20). It also helps us understand Paul's exhortation to "pray at all times *in the Spirit,* with all prayer and supplication" (6:18). This kind of prayer responds to a certain need and fills a vacuum in Christian prayer, i.e., spontaneous communal prayer. Liturgical prayer is communal but not spontaneous; private prayer is spontaneous but not communal. There are times in which we can pray spontaneously as the Spirit leads, but we share our prayer with others, combining our various gifts and charisms and being built up by the fervor of others, putting together the different "tongues of fire" in such a way as to make a single flame.

We have a wonderful example of spontaneous communal prayer in Acts 4. Peter and John, released from prison and charged not to speak in the name of Jesus, return to their community, and everyone begins to pray. At the end all are filled again with the power of the Spirit and continue to preach Christ "with *parresia*" ("with boldness"). I know pastors who, in difficult situations, have learned to do what Peter and John did that day: they call their community together and pray with them—believers with believers—or they kneel and invite the faithful to pray over them.

Prayer groups, like all human activities, are not exempt from dangers and flaws of various kinds, but on the whole they are something new that should be received with "thanksgiving and consolation," as *Lumen gentium* says of charisms in general.[10]

4. Creation Returns to You

We understand by now that prayer, especially trinitarian prayer or prayer in the Spirit, is indispensable for growing in holiness. It unites us to God, who alone is "the Holy One" and "the fountain of all holiness." The sacraments and the word also unite us to God, but prayer does so in its own inimitable way: through desire.

Desire is the soul of prayer. People's desire is their prayer, says Augustine; if desire continues, then prayer continues, and people who wish for prayer to continue should never cease desiring.[11] A beautiful prayer that is recited during the third ordinary day of the first week in Lent says, "help us to grow in our desire for you" or, literally translated, "make us shine in desiring you."[12] It is as though God shows himself from heaven and catches sight on earth of luminous points of various brightness according to the intensity of desire that each one has for him. Isaiah exclaims, "O LORD, we wait for thee; thy memorial name is the desire of our soul" (26:8). The psalms are models of prayer precisely because they are permeated by this sense of desire or yearning for God.

Prayer anticipates the return of creatures to God and is thus

an eschatological activity that anticipates the end, the fulfillment of all things. A great fourteenth-century Flemish mystic
wrote, "God is a flowing and ebbing sea which ceaselessly flows
out into all his beloved according to their needs and merits and
which flows back with all those upon whom he has bestowed
his gifts in heaven and on earth."[13] This suggests the image of
a sea that flows onto the beach at high tide and draws into
itself whatever is on the beach with its receding waves. Some
boats, however, are bounded on all sides or tied to a post in the
ground. The sea surrounds them and caresses them, as though
inviting them to follow. For a little while, the boats are lifted up
and float, but since they are tied, they do not follow the sea as it
recedes. They stay on shore, while other boats that are not tied
put out into the deep under the sun on the tranquil sea.

This is what happens with the Trinity. The Trinity sends out
its word and its grace like a beneficial wave that envelops people and invites them to follow into its immensity. Some souls
are "untied," ready, and they follow with joy. Others, instead,
are tied by the ropes of old habits, by worldly attachments, or
by fear of the unknown. For a moment they let themselves be
lifted up and gently rocked, but when it comes time to decide to
go forward, they do not feel like going, and they stay on land.
What will happen to them? Will they one day know the intoxi-
cation of the open sea, or will they be like the boats that stay on
the shore and become corroded by sea salt?

The cry of Christ that the pope has echoed in the letter with
which he opened the new millennium resounds here more than
ever: "*Duc in altum,* put out into the deep!"[14] Hoist the sails, lift
the anchors! Do not be afraid of venturing forth into the open
sea of holiness.

There has been a wide diffusion of liturgical hymns composed by Trappist nuns in Vitorchiano and Valserena in central Italy. There is one among them for vespers of great theological profundity and lyric inspiration that wonderfully conveys the sentiment that I have tried to evoke. Let us read it to conclude our meditation on trinitarian prayer on a doxological note (as is fitting).

O infinite Trinity,
We sing of your glory in this evening prayer,
Because through Christ you have made us sons
And our hearts your dwelling place.

Eternal, beyond time,
The fountain of the life that never dies,
Creation returns to you
In a never-ending stream of love.

We sing to you, O Immense One,
In this brief Sabbath of time
That heralds the great day without night
In which we will see you as living light.

We give our praise to you,
O most sweet and blessed Trinity,
Which always flows forth and always flows back
In the calm sea of your own Love.
Amen.[15]

1. Pope John Paul II, *Novo millennio ineunte* [At the Beginning of the New Millennium], 31 (Boston: Pauline Media and Books, 2001), p. 42.

2. Pope John Paul II, 31, p. 43.

3. Pope John Paul II, 32, p. 44.

4. Blessed Angela of Foligno, *Instructions*, II, in *Angela of Foligno: Complete Works*, pref. by Romana Guarnieri, trans. by Paul Lachance, OFM (New York: Paulist Press, 1993), pp. 235–36.

5. Augustine, *Commentary on the First Epistle of John,* 7, 8, trans. by John W. Rettig, vol. 92 in *The Fathers of the Church* (Washington, DC: The Catholic University of America Press, 1995), p. 223.

6. Pope John Paul II, 32, p. 44.

7. See Irenaeus of Lyons, *Against Heresies*, IV, 7, 4; V, 5, 2; 15, 2–3; 16, 1; 28, 4, trans. by A. Cleveland Coxe, vol. 1 in *The Ante-Nicene Fathers*, ed. by Alexander Roberts and James Donaldson (New York: Charles Scribner's Sons, 1926), p. 470; p. 531; p. 543; p. 544; p. 557.

8. "Eucharistic Prayer IV," in *The Sacramentary* (New York: Catholic Book Publishing Co., 1985).

9. Basil of Caesarea, *On the Holy Spirit*, XXVI, 62, trans. by Blomfield Jackson, vol. 8 in *Nicene and Post-Nicene Fathers*, ed. Philip Schaff and Henry Wace (Grand Rapids, MI: William B. Eerdmans Publishing Co., 1956), p. 39.

10. *Lumen gentium* [Dogmatic Constitution on the Church], 12, in *The Documents of Vatican II*, gen. ed. Walter M. Abbott, SJ, intro. by Cardinal Lawrence Shehan, trans. by Joseph Gallagher (New York: Herder and Herder Association Press, 1966), p. 30.

11. See Augustine, *Tractates on the Gospel of John*, 40, 10, trans. by John W. Rettig, vol. 88 of *the Fathers of the Church* (Washington, DC: The Catholic University of America Press, 1993), p. 133; see *Commentary on the First Epistle of John*, 4, 6; "Exposition of Psalm 37," 14, in *Exposition of the Psalms 33–50*, vol. 3 of Part III, trans. by Maria Boulding, OSB, *The Works of St. Augustine*, ed. by John E. Rotelle, OSA (Hyde Park, NJ: New City Press, 2000), p. 156; "Letter 130," 10, 20, vol. 18, trans. by Wilfrid Parsons, SND, in *The Fathers of the Church* (New York: Fathers of the Church, Inc., 1953), pp. 390–91.

12. Roman Missal, First Week of Lent, Tuesday (*desiderio tui fulgeat*).

13. John Ruusbroec, *The Spiritual Espousals*, 41, in *The Spiritual Espousals and Other Works*, pref. by Louis Dupré, trans. by James A. Wiseman, OSB (New York: Paulist Press, 1985), p. 103.

14. Pope John Paul II, 1, p. 7.

15. Published in *I salmi, preghiera cristiana* [*Psalms, Christian Prayer*], ed. by Paolino Beltrame Quattrocchi (Naples: Edizioni del deserto, 1977), p. 420.

Chapter 4

"Being a Trinity, God Is Nonetheless Simple"[1]: CONTEMPLATING THE TRINITY TO OVERCOME THE HATEFUL HYPOCRISY OF THE WORLD

A popular iconographic tradition depicts St. Augustine watching a child on the seashore who is scooping water from the sea in a seashell and pouring it into a small hole he has dug in the sand. We know the legend that inspired it: Augustine was beginning to write a treatise on the Trinity. By means of that incident, the Christ Child, or an angel sent by God, wants him to understand one thing: just as it is impossible to pour the ocean into a small hole in the sand, so too it is impossible to contain the Trinity in the human mind by the feeble instrument of reason. Augustine will continue to write his sublime pages on the Trinity, but he will be very conscious (and he repeats it often) that what he is writing on every page is only drops of water compared to the sea.

This will always be the case in any discussion of the Trinity: it is an attempt to draw water from a boundless and bottomless ocean with a seashell.

1. The Trinity and Divine Simplicity

Augustine experienced one of the happiest "immersions" in the sea of the Trinity the day he formulated the clear principle of divine simplicity upon which his doctrine of the Trinity is chiefly based; and the Latin church followed him on this point. Augustine says,

> This Trinity is one God. And, although it is a Trinity, it is nonetheless simple. . . . Our reason for calling it simple is because it is what it has. . . . For, it is true that the Father *has* a Son, yet He *is* not the Son. And the Son *has* a Father, yet *is* not the Father. Therefore, as regards Himself, without reference to His relation with the others, the Father is what he has. Thus, when He is said to be living, we mean that He has life and is the very life He has.[2]

The dogmatic formulation of this insight, which comes from the Council of Florence in 1442, is that in God "everything . . . is one where there is no opposition of relationship."[3] (*In Deo omnia sunt communia ubi non obviat relationis oppositio.*)

This principle firmly establishes the simplicity of God once and for all. Augustine says, "Nor because he is three must we think of him as triple, or three by multiplication."[4] The Trinity does not destroy the simplicity of God, because simplicity has to do with nature, and the nature (absolute being) of God is one and simple. St. Thomas Aquinas faithfully takes up this doctrinal inheritance, making simplicity the primary attribute of God.[5]

This is the theological formulation of a truth that the Bible expresses in a concrete way through images: "God is light and in him is no darkness at all" (1 John 1:5). The absence of any kind of mixture is also one of the several meanings of the divine title *Qadosh,* "Holy." Absolute fullness, absolute simplicity.

The great mystic St. Catherine of Genoa designates this aspect of the divine nature that she loved with the words "clear" and "clarity," words that simultaneously indicate purity and wholeness together, fullness and absolute homogeneity. God is "all of one piece."

The doctrine of the Trinity, then, saves—not compromises—divine simplicity. That simplicity is destroyed in doctrines like those in ancient gnosticism that imagine a divine world populated by beings (the *aeons*) of varying perfection in conflict with one another. According to them, there is an element of darkness and error hidden within the divine world itself that will in the end determine the existence of evil in the world and even of the world itself.

The simplicity of God is also challenged today by certain perspectives in so-called depth psychology derived from Carl Jung. With an approach that resembles that of heretical gnosticism, it stretches the boundaries of good and evil until the two poles move closer to each other and overlap, with the result that evil is seen as nothing more than "the other face of reality," and the devil as nothing more than "God's shadow." Light and darkness, good and evil, the creative principle and the destructive principle, become nothing more than two sides of the same coin on all levels of reality, including the divine.

Along this line, an author widely read some years ago by students of psychology ended up accusing Christianity of introducing "the perverse contraposition of good and evil." He wrote, "Christianity likes the childish mind, it is a religion of the *child* archetype, so it stresses being *simple,* which means originally being single not subtle [emphasis mine]."[6]

St. Augustine asked himself what people did when they did

not succeed at resisting vices (or were unwilling to resist them). They simply attributed them to God! And that is why they made a god out of lust, Venus; a god out of violence, Mars; and so on, feeling themselves thus justified in practicing the same vices. If we do not want to repeat that same ingenuous procedure, we should not try to transfer our complexity onto God, but rather imitate his simplicity.

For us, simplicity is always something we set out to attain, and never our starting point. God is simple by nature; we are by nature complex at all levels: metaphysical, psychological, and moral. God's attributes are identified with his being, but that is not the case for us. God's appearance—his manifestation outside of himself—is always infinitely inferior to his being. For us, unfortunately, just the opposite is true: our appearance tends to be superior to our being.

God's simplicity is "pure, unadulterated fullness." As the Scripture says, "nothing can be added or taken away" from him (Sirach 42:21). Insofar as he is the height of *fullness*, nothing *can* be added to him; insofar as he is the height of *purity*, nothing *should* be taken away. In us the two things are never united; one contradicts the other. Our purity is always obtained by taking something away, purifying ourselves, "remov[ing] the evil of our actions" (see Isaiah 1:16). In this respect, holiness resembles sculpture. Leonardo da Vinci used to define sculpture as "the art of taking away," because a piece of sculpture is created not by adding something (color to color in painting, note to note in music, stone to stone in architecture) but by removing something. The sculptor chips off superfluous parts with his chisel so that the desired image can emerge.

2. Authentic Persons or Fictive Characters?

Having proposed the Trinity as the "high standard"[7] for Christian life, we look to see what we should "remove" from ourselves to approach the simplicity of the Trinity. The answer is obvious: we should remove the culpable duplicity that the Bible calls hypocrisy. The aim of this present reflection is "contemplating the Trinity to overcome the hateful hypocrisy of the world."

Jesus called hypocrisy a leaven, "the leaven of the Pharisees" (Luke 12:1). It really is a leaven that "leavens the whole lump" (1 Corinthians 5:6), that is, it can corrupt all our actions, not only evil ones, but also, and especially, good ones.

It is surprising how this sin—the one most denounced by God in the Bible and by Christ in the gospels—so rarely enters into our ordinary examinations of conscience. The greatest act of hypocrisy would be to hide hypocrisy—to hide it from ourselves, of course, because it is impossible to hide it from God. "If we say we have no sin [let us indeed add hypocrisy], we deceive ourselves, and the truth is not in us. If we confess our sins, he is faithful and just, and will forgive our sins and cleanse us from all unrighteousness" (1 John 1:8-9). Hypocrisy is largely overcome at the very moment it is recognized.

Every person, wrote Blaise Pascal, has two lives: one is the true life, and the other is the imaginary life lived in one's own or others' opinion. We work tirelessly to embellish and preserve our imaginary selves, and we neglect our true selves. If we have some virtue or some merit, we take great pains to make it known, in one way or another, to enhance our imaginary self by it. We are ready to diminish our true selves to add to our imaginary selves, even to the point of being cowardly if it would make us seem courageous, and even to giving up our life provided that people would talk about it.[8]

To resist hypocrisy better, we can try to discover the origin and significance of that term. The word comes from the language of theater. At the beginning it simply meant "recitation, acting on stage." The intrinsic element of falsehood that occurs in every stage representation did not go unnoticed by the ancients in spite of its acknowledged high moral and artistic value. This was the source of the negative judgment on the acting profession, restricted during certain periods to slaves and even directly prohibited by the Christian apologists. The sorrow and the joy represented and emphasized are not real sorrow and real joy but appearance, a fiction. The exterior words and attitudes do not correspond to the inner reality of the heart.

We use the word "fiction" in a neutral or even a positive sense. (It is a literary and entertainment genre that is very popular today!) The ancients gave it the sense that it really has: make-believe. What was negative in stage fiction was transferred to the word "hypocrisy." After originally being a neutral term, it became one of the few words with an exclusively negative meaning. There are those who brag about being proud or dissolute, but no one brags about being a hypocrite.

The origin of the word puts us on track to discover the nature of hypocrisy. It is turning life into a stage where we perform for the public; it means putting on a mask and ceasing to be a person in order to become a character. Someone once wrote anonymously on the difference between the two:

A fictive character is nothing but the corruption of an authentic person. A person has a face; a character wears a mask. A person is completely naked; a character is completely clothed. A person loves authenticity and reality; a character lives a life of fiction and artifice. A person follows his or her own convictions; a character follows a script. A person interprets life as a journey through a desert; a character only knows the small space of a stage. A person is humble and gentle; a character is cumbersome and unwieldy.

This innate tendency in human beings has been increased dramatically by the current culture, which is dominated by images, the film industry, and especially television. René Descartes said, *Cogito, ergo sum,* "I think, therefore I am." Today that tends to be substituted by "I appear, therefore, I am." A famous French moralist defined hypocrisy as "a homage vice pays to virtue."[9] In our world today, we see a kind of upside-down hypocrisy. People invent sins they did not commit so as not to seem less free and open-minded than others. Young men and women brag about escapades that, fortunately, they have not experienced, so as not to seem better than their companions. Hypocrisy, says Bruce Marshall in one of his novels, has now become the homage that virtue pays to vice.

Unfortunately, along with this upside-down hypocrisy, the old hypocrisy that is a trap, especially for pious and religious people, also continues to exist. A rabbi during the time of Christ said that 90 percent of the hypocrisy in the world could be found in Jerusalem.[10] The reason is simple: Wherever spiritual values, piety, and virtues are most highly esteemed, the strongest temptation is to pretend to have them—so as not to seem to be without them.

Another danger comes from the multitude of rituals that pious people are supposed to perform and the rules they are supposed to observe. If these rituals are not accompanied by a continuous effort to establish them within one's soul by means of love for God and neighbor, they become empty shells. St. Paul, speaking of external rites and precepts, says, "These have indeed an appearance of wisdom in promoting rigor of devotion and self-abasement and severity to the body, but they are of no value in checking the indulgence of the flesh" (Colossians 2:23). In this case, says the apostle, people are "holding the form of religion but denying the power of it" (2 Timothy 3:5).

If we ask why hypocrisy is such an abomination to the Lord, the answer is clear. Hypocrisy unseats God, puts him in second place, because creatures—the audience—are put in first place. It is as though someone in the presence of a king turns his back on him in order to focus attention only on the servants. "Man looks on the outward appearance, but the LORD looks on the heart" (1 Samuel 16:7). To cultivate outward appearance more than the heart automatically means giving more importance to human beings than to God.

Hypocrisy, then, is essentially a lack of faith, a form of idolatry in which creatures are given the place of the Creator. Jesus attributes this to his enemies' lack of ability to believe in him: "How can you believe, who receive glory from one another and do not seek the glory that comes from the only God?" (John 5:44).

Hypocrisy is also a lack of charity toward one's neighbor, because it tends to reduce brothers and sisters to admirers. It does not recognize the dignity that is properly theirs, because it sees others only in relation to one's own image.

Rublev, Andrei (1360–c.1430)
Icon of the Old Testament Trinity, c.1410
Tretyakov Gallery, Moscow, Russia
Scala / Art Resource, NY

Masaccio (Maso di San Giovanni) (1401–1428)
The Trinity, fresco, full view. c. 1425. Post-restoration
S. Maria Novella, Florence, Italy
Scala / Art Resource, NY

The Holy Trinity (15th century)
The Novgorod School
Russian Museum, St. Petersburg
The Bridgeman Art Library

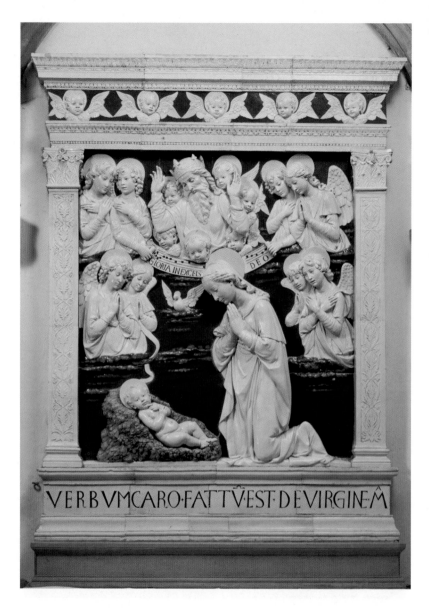

Robbia, Andrea della (1435–1525)
Nativity
Sanctuary, La Verna, Italy
Scala / Art Resource, NY

Christ's judgment on hypocrisy is like a flaming sword: "They have received their reward" (Matthew 6:2). They already have a signed receipt; they cannot expect anything more. It is a reward, moreover, that is illusory and counterproductive even on the human level. It has been said, and it is true, that glory flees the one who pursues it and pursues the one who flees it.

The worst thing one can do after hearing or reading a description of hypocrisy is to use it to judge others. It is precisely those people to whom Jesus applies the name of hypocrites: "You hypocrite, first take the log out of your own eye, and then you will see clearly to take the speck out of your brother's eye" (Matthew 7:5).

3. The Unleavened Bread of Sincerity

Let us look at the ideal and the cure that the Word of God gives for hypocrisy: "Cleanse out the old leaven that you may be a new lump, as you really are unleavened. For Christ, our paschal lamb, has been sacrificed. Let us, therefore, celebrate the festival, not with the old leaven, the leaven of malice and evil, but *with the unleavened bread of sincerity and truth*" (1 Corinthians 5:7-8).

It seems that this text was written as the Passover celebration was approaching. The feast that the apostle invites people to celebrate is not, then, just any feast but the feast par excellence, the only feast that Christianity recognized in the first three centuries of its history—Easter, the Christian Passover. In this passage we have the first undeniable mention of the existence of a Christian feast of Passover.

On the eve of the Passover, the thirteenth day of Nisan, the Jewish ritual required the housewife to scour the whole house by candlelight, cleaning every corner to remove even the smallest vestige of leavened bread so as to celebrate the Passover the next day with only unleavened bread. (Leaven was synonymous for the Jews with corruption, and unleavened bread was a symbol of purity, newness, and integrity.) This is the origin of the tradition of a thorough spring cleaning.

St. Paul sees this as a significant metaphor for all of Christian life. Christ has been sacrificed; he is the true Passover, which the ancient Passover foreshadowed. We need, then, to scour our inner homes, our hearts, and remove everything that is old and corrupt in order to become "a new lump." We too need to do a thorough spring cleaning.

The most interesting word used by the apostle here is "sincerity." This is a translation of the Greek word *eilikrineia* (from *eile*, "the radiance of the sun," and *krino*, "to judge"). It refers to something that has been examined in the light of the sun and found pure, something that has radiant transparency. (From the same verb, *krino*, come two opposite words: hypocrisy and transparency!)

I know a nice fairy tale called "The Glass Country." It tells about a person who is magically transported to a country entirely made of glass: glass houses, glass birds, glass trees, people who are like lovely glass figurines. Yet nothing has ever been broken or shattered, because all the people have learned to move very gently in order not to harm one another. People encountering each other answer questions before they are even asked, because thoughts have also become open and transparent. No one tries to lie anymore, knowing that everyone can read his or her thoughts.

The protagonist becomes accustomed to this new life very

quickly. When one day he is made to return to the real world, he is upset and exclaims, "But I cannot live in a country that is not made of glass! I need people to be sincere, I need things to be transparent, I need gentle gestures and voices."[11] He resigns himself only when the person who had orchestrated his transport tells him, "Your task now is to live here like you lived in the Glass Country and to 'infect' others, making them like the inhabitants of that country."

The true country of glass (or rather crystal, according to Revelation) is heaven, where everyone is transparent, and there is nothing hidden and nothing to hide. But we need to begin to live down here as they do in the heavenly Jerusalem. To live as if our thoughts were open and clear to everyone—they are at least to one person, God!—and as if our speech could not hide or falsify our thoughts. Let us try to imagine for a moment what our life together would be like in our families, our religious communities, our church. . . . Perhaps it sends shivers down our spines just to think about it, but it would be very healthy to make ourselves try to do it.

If hypocrisy consists of making a show of the good that one does not do, an effective remedy to counteract this tendency is to conceal the good that one does. To do so would be to prefer those hidden acts, unspoiled by any earthly gaze, that save all their perfume for God. St. John of the Cross says,

More pleasing to God is one good work, howsoever small it be, that is done in secret with no desire that it shall be known than a thousand that are done with the desire that they may be known of men. . . . A good work performed in purity and singleness of heart, for God's sake, in a breast that is pure, makes a kingdom of singleness of heart for him that performs it.[12]

Jesus repeatedly recommends this kind of approach: "Pray in secret . . . fast in secret . . . give alms in secret . . . and your Father who sees in secret will reward you" (see Matthew 6:2-18). These are subtle actions in our relationship with God that invigorate the soul.

It is not a question of making a rigid rule about all this. Jesus also says, "Let your light so shine before men, that they may see your good works and give glory to your Father who is in heaven" (Matthew 5:16). It is a question of discerning when it is good for others to see and when it is better that they do not.

4. Mary, the Earthly Reflection of Divine Simplicity

We have a reflection on earth of trinitarian simplicity: Mary. Throughout the gospels she appears as simplicity personified. One of the most beautiful praises of Our Lady's simplicity is from Martin Luther's commentary on the Magnificat:

The wondrous pure spirit of Mary is worthy of even greater praise, because, having such overwhelming honors heaped upon her head, she does not let them tempt her, but acts as though she did not see it, remains, "even and right in the way," clings only to God's goodness, . . . overlooks the good things she does feel, and neither takes pleasure nor seeks her own enjoyment in it. Thus she can truly sing, "My spirit rejoices in God, my Savior."[13]

Mary has perfected Pauline *eilikrineia,* paschal transparency; her life is one of radiant transparency.

Let us ask her to obtain for us the gift from God to become, as her Son exhorts us, "innocent as doves," even when one's duty or office requires that we be "wise as serpents" (Matthew 10:16).

Let us finish again this time with a prayer, one from Psalm 139: "O Lord, thou hast searched me and known me!" If hypocrisy is more concerned with people's approval than with God's, here we find the remedy for it. To pray this psalm is like allowing oneself to be X-rayed. A person can sense coming beneath God's gaze bit by bit, but in the end the person who is praying comes to love this light and joyfully exclaims, "Search me, O God, and know my heart!"

O Lord, thou hast searched me and known me!
Thou knowest when I sit down and when I rise up;
    thou discernest my thoughts from afar.
Thou searchest out my path and my lying down,
    and art acquainted with all my ways.
Even before a word is on my tongue,
    lo, O Lord, thou knowest it altogether.
. . . .
Whither shall I go from thy Spirit?
    Or whither shall I flee from thy presence?
If I ascend to heaven, thou art there!
    If I make my bed in Sheol, thou art there!
If I take the wings of the morning
    and dwell in the uttermost parts of the sea,
even there thy hand shall lead me,

and thy right hand shall hold me.
If I say, "let only darkness cover me,
    and the light about me be night,"
even the darkness is not dark to thee,
    the night is bright as the day;
    for darkness is as light with thee.

. . . .

Search me, O GOD, and know my heart!
    Try me and know my thoughts!
And see if there be any wicked way in me,
    and lead me in the way everlasting!

Yes, Lord, see if we are walking in any wicked ways and lead us in the way of simplicity and transparency. Amen.

1. See Augustine, *The City of God*, XI, 10, trans. by Gerald G. Walsh, SJ, et al. (New York: Image Books, 1958), p. 321.

2. Augustine, *The City of God*, XI, 10, p. 321.

3. "The Council of Florence, 1442," in Josef Neuner, SJ, and Jacques Dupuis, SJ, *The Christian Faith in the Doctrinal Documents of the Catholic Church*, ed. by Jacques Dupuis, SJ, 7th ed. rev. (New York: Alba House, 2001), p. 156.

4. Augustine, *The Trinity* , VI, 2, 9, trans. by Edmund Hill, OP, vol. 5 in *The Works of Saint Augustine,* ed. by John E. Rotelle, OSA (Brooklyn, NY: New City Press, 1991), p. 211.

5. See Thomas Aquinas, "Whether God Is Altogether Simple," I, q. 3, a. 7, *Summa Theologica*, vol. 1, trans. by Fathers of the English Dominican Province (Westminster, MD: Christian Classics, 1981), p. 19.

6. James Hillman, *Interviews: Conversations with Laura Pozzo on Psychotherapy, Biography, Love, Soul, Dreams, Work, Imagination, and the State of the Culture* (New York: Harper & Row, 1983), p. 86.

7. Pope John Paul II, *Novo millennio ineunte* [At the Beginning of the New Millennium], 31 (Boston: Pauline Media and Books, 2001), p. 42.

8. See Blaise Pascal, *Pensées*, 147, intro. by T. S. Eliot, trans. by W. F. Trotter (Franklin, PA: The Franklin Library, 1979), p. 47.

9. "L'hypocrisie est un homage que le vice rend à la vertue" (François de la Rochefoucauld, *Maxims*, 208, trans. and intro. by Stuart D. Warner and Stéphane Douard [South Bend, IN: St. Augustine's Press, 2001], p. 43).

10. See Hermann L. Strack and Paul Billerbeck, *Das Evangelium nach Matthäus* [*The Gospel According to Matthew*] (Munich: C. H. Beck'sche Verlagsbuchhandlung, 1926), vol. 1, p. 718.

11. Lauretta, *Il bosco dei lillà* [*The Forest of Lilacs*] (Milan: Ancora, 1994), p. 90ff.

12. John of the Cross, *Spiritual Sentences and Maxims*, 20, 2, in *The Complete Works of Saint John of the Cross*, vol. 2, trans. by E. Allison Peers (Westminster, MD: Newman Press, 1949), p. 243.

13. Martin Luther, Commentary on the Magnificat, 7, trans. by A. T. W. Steinhaeuser, vol. 21 of *Luther's* Works, ed. by Jaroslav Pelikan (St. Louis, MO: Concordia Publishing House, 1956), p. 311.

Chapter 5

"You Are Beauty":
CONTEMPLATING THE TRINITY TO
OVERCOME THE ALLURE OF FALSE BEAUTY

1. Trinitarian Beauty

The church fathers have said some wonderful things about divine beauty. Its loftiest celebration comes from Dionysius the Aeropagite when he speaks of the divine names:

> God, who is beautiful beyond being, is said to be Beauty—
> for it gives Beauty from itself in a manner appropriate to
> each. . . . [He is] the *productive cause* which makes and
> conserves the whole by its love of the beauty which is
> proper for each being; the *final cause*—for all beings merge
> for the sake of the beautiful; the *paradigmatic cause* [for]
> all are determined according to it.[1]

This eulogy to beauty has a serious limitation, however. It deals with the beauty of God's *essence* and not with God's *personal* beauty. Dionysius says it explicitly: the attribute of beauty, like those of goodness and wisdom, expresses the relationship between God and the creation (with God as the cause and transcendent model of every kind of beauty). In the Platonic tradition it applies, therefore, to divinity in general, not to the individual Persons; it is *divine* beauty but not exactly *trinitarian* beauty.

Let us take a further step and speak of trinitarian beauty in the strict sense. If God is beautiful, he must be so for someone who is eternal, just as he is. Just as there is no music where there is no ear to hear it, so too there is no beauty where there is no eye to admire it. But for whom would God be beautiful if there were no Trinity? For creatures? In that case he would be beautiful only from the time the world began to exist, not to mention the fact that no creature is capable of fully perceiving divine beauty that is infinite and transcendent.

Beauty is an attribute of a person, even more than it is of nature. The divine Persons are beautiful. The Father is beautiful to the Son, as the Son is beautiful to the Father, who finds in the Son "all his pleasure." In God there is a fatherly beauty and a filial beauty. The same must be said of the Breath they share, who is the Spirit. The Son is presented to us in Scripture in eternal contemplation of the beauty (the "glory") of the Father, and "He reflects the glory of God" (Hebrews 1:3).

In the Trinity God loves himself without any shadow of egotism and admires himself without any shadow of narcissism.

Trinitarian beauty is a wide area to explore. It is, like the Persons themselves, a beauty of relationship. It consists in beautiful relationships: it is the synthesis between unity and diversity. The least inadequate images of this beauty are from music and dance. In musical harmony, every note derives its beauty from its relationship to the other notes. When a man and woman dance together, every movement derives its beauty through each partner's coordination with the movement of the other. Beauty is the three divine Persons facing each other from the beginning with a joyful and silent gaze.

This is the beauty that Rublëv succeeded in portraying in his famous icon of the Trinity: a beauty that emanates from the very relationship of each Person to the other, from the meeting of their gazes and the recollection of their movements. It is a beauty of relationship that is not static but dynamic. One can reproduce each of the three figures of the icon separately (which is sometimes done), but that breaks the enchantment and loses the power of the whole.

Beauty has always been something that is impossible to define. One can say about beauty what Augustine said about time: "What, then, is time? If no one asks me, I know; if I want to explain it to someone who asks me, I do not know."[2] Perhaps we can understand something more about it if we begin with its original form in the Trinity as a beauty of relationship. Every Christian presentation about God should have a trinitarian character; in this regard there is still much to be done.

2. "Beauty is Vain"[3]

Only now can we begin to consider divine beauty in relationship to the world, as Dionysius did in his text. He called the Trinity "Wise and Beautiful" because of whom all beings "are filled with every divine harmony and sacred good [beautiful] form."[4]

To say that God is the author of beauty not only means that he created all the beautiful things in the world but that he also created the very sense of beauty, putting a love for it and a capacity to recognize it in the hearts of human beings, which we call the aesthetic sense. He wanted beauty (together with goodness) to be a ladder on which we ascend to him, the "one who attracts," the magnet.

But if this is the case, how does beauty so often lead to destruction, and why do we read such things in Scripture as "beauty is vain" (Proverbs 31:30), "beauty has deceived you" (Daniel 13:56), and "your heart was proud because of your beauty" (Ezekiel 28:17)?

That is the issue I want to focus on in this meditation. I do not want to deal with the theme of beauty from the *essential and metaphysical* point of view—what beauty is in itself, what its relationship to truth and goodness is—but from an *existential* point of view. In other words, I would like to reflect on our experience of beauty. I would also like to highlight a very specific and limited aspect of that experience: not the beauty of seas and sunsets but of the human body, male and female. This is the beauty that generates *eros,* one of the great forces that moves the world—and perhaps the most powerful. The beauty of seas and sunsets is not erotic, but the beauty of the body is, with all that we know it entails. This is true whether in life or art. Even in response to art, people visiting the Uffizi Gallery in Florence react differently to a landscape or a still life than to Sandro Botticelli's Venus.

To the extent in which advertising or entertainment reflect the spirit, the tastes, and the expectations of an age (and to a large extent they do), this type of beauty that I referred to as erotic seems to be the most sought-after value, the great "object of worship" in affluent societies. To prove that, we only need to think of fashion shows, calendars of nudes, and the role assigned to women in the world of entertainment and advertising. Modern man "doubts the truth, resists the good, but is fascinated by beauty."[5]

This is a new challenge for believers. It is first of all a *human problem,* whose solution will determine the very future of culture and life.

For us at this time, however, it is above all a *spiritual problem:* how do we live the beatitude about purity of heart that the gospel presents to all believers in an environment so saturated with sensuality? External defenses used in the past no longer work: cloisters, religious habits, and rules. . . . Modern media have bypassed all these defenses and assault us outside and inside our homes. We need to strengthen our internal defenses, our strong personal convictions founded on God's word and on right reason.

This is also a *problem for proclamation.* How do we evangelize by means of beauty a world that has such a debased idea of it?

3. The Ambiguity of Beauty

The words of the Idiot, one of Dostoevsky's favorite characters, are well known and often repeated: "Beauty will save the world"; however, that affirmation is followed by a question: "What kind of beauty will save the world?"[6] It is clear—for him as well—that not every beautiful thing will save the world. There is a beauty that can save the world, and a beauty that can lead it to perdition.

"God," writes Paul Evdokimov, "is not the only one who 'clothes himself in beauty.' Evil imitates him in this respect and thus makes beauty a profoundly ambiguous quality."[7] There has been an evolution in this regard from the medieval to the modern era. In the Middle Ages, it was assumed that the good was beautiful and evil was ugly, but that is no longer the case. The devil, who was represented in figurative arts and poetry

(Dante!) as grotesque and monstrous, began at a certain point to be represented as beautiful or at least as melancholic and poetic. Some painters (for example, Lorenzo Lotto in a painting in the Loreto Museum in central Italy) depict the devil as a very handsome youth, more like "Lucifer," a luminous star, than as "an angel of darkness." In poetry, as well, starting with John Milton, the devil takes on an aspect of fallen beauty. Beauty is no longer an exclusive attribute of the good.

One sign of the ambiguity about beauty is that we find in modern culture, along with its exaltation, an explicit refusal of beauty, a real "insult to beauty," so much so that we can speak of the death of beauty as we did in the past about the death of God. Since those in the past who expressed themselves about beauty were almost exclusively men, the disdain for beauty was transferred to a disdain for woman. In the works of the fathers of modern so-called poetry we find such terrible verses as "O sweet merciful Woman—but a heap of entrails. . . ."[8]

In a painting an artist depicts monstrous birds rushing toward a female body as if it were a corpse. Someone has described some of the famous women of abstract art as "corpses of beauty."[9]

It is beauty itself (and not just that of woman) that becomes "demystified" and violated in this way. The beginning of a collection of poems by Arthur Rimbaud is famous: "One night I settled Beauty on my knee.—And I found her bitter.—And I insulted her."[10] In art this attitude leads to the controversial depiction of anti-aesthetic objects like urinals and other similar things that have ended up in some museums.

What causes this ambiguity? The traditional answer is "sin." But according to the biblical account, the ambiguity of beauty was not only the effect of sin but also its cause. Eve was seduced precisely by the beauty of the forbidden fruit, whatever the fruit may have signified. Eve saw that the fruit was "a delight to the eyes" (Genesis 3:6). It was aesthetically beautiful. People would not turn away from God if they were not attracted to created things. There are two elements present in every sin: a turning from God and a turning to creatures or created things (*aversio a Deo et conversio ad creaturas*), and the latter psychologically precedes the former.

Thus, there is an anterior cause to sin itself. The ambiguity of beauty finds its roots in the composite nature of human beings, who have both a material and an immaterial element, something that draws them to multiplicity and something that inclines them instead to unity. It is the same God who created both together in a profound "substantial" unity, because with the exercise of free will guided by the word of God, people choose the direction in which they will develop, i.e., whether "upward" toward that which is "above" them or "downward" toward that which is "below" them, toward unity or multiplicity.

The dignity of human beings and the privileged exercise of their freedom consist precisely in this capacity for self-determination. In creating a human being free, writes a Renaissance philosopher, it is as though God says,

> I have placed thee at the center of the world, that from there thou mayest more conveniently look around and see whatsoever is in the world. Neither heavenly nor earthly, neither mortal nor immortal have We made thee. Thou, like a judge appointed for being honorable, art the molder and maker of thyself; thou mayest sculpt thyself into whatever shape thou dost prefer. Thou canst grow downward

into the lower nature which are brutes. Thou canst again grow upward from thy soul's reason into the higher natures which are divine.[11]

This explains the struggle between flesh and the Spirit, as well as the dramatic element that characterizes the existence of human beings in the world and their relationship to beauty.

In the 1977 earthquake in Assisi, a fresco by Giovanni Cimabue in the dome of the upper basilica was destroyed and shattered into thousands of miniscule colored fragments. There is a painstaking process underway now to reassemble those pieces to reconstruct the original fresco. This is a depiction of what happens when we shift from the uncreated Beauty of God to the multiplicity of beautiful things in the world. The beauty that we experience in the world is *fragmented.*

Sin begins, with respect to beauty, when one forgets the whole and becomes attached to the fragment. To return to the analogy, if someone finds a fragment and steals or destroys it instead of making it part of the reconstruction of the original fresco, that endangers the whole project. When people do not relate to created beauty as a springboard to lift themselves up to incorruptible Beauty with praise and desire but instead rush toward it, then they make the momentary pleasure an end in itself, "and upon the shapely things you have made I rushed headlong, I, misshapen, . . . [to] those things which would have no being were they not in you."[12]

Created beauty becomes then the tomb instead of the occasion of exercising freedom, because, as we know, it enslaves people. To possess and enjoy that beauty, some people do exactly what others do in order to get drugs: steal, kill, or kill themselves. In crimes of passion we take into account the extenuating circumstances precisely because we realize that the person is operating with reduced freedom. Disordered love of beauty leads to "beastly conduct," because it deprives people of the very things that make them "human"—reason and freedom.

Literature offers us famous symbols of these two kinds of feminine beauty—beauty that elevates and beauty that destroys—in Dante's Beatrice and Homer's Helen. The ambiguity of beauty also finds memorable expression in the Bible. On the one hand, there is the beauty in the Song of Songs of the two lovers trying to outdo each other in celebrating one another; on the other hand, there is the beauty of a woman that drew David into adultery and crime (see 2 Samuel 11:2). "Beauty has deceived you," says Daniel to one of the two elders who wanted the chaste Susanna put to death (see Daniel 13:56).

Stopping at created beauty is seen by the Bible as the very essence of idolatry, insofar as it puts the creature in the place of the Creator:

> For all men who were ignorant of God were foolish by
> nature;
> and they were unable from the good things that are seen
> to know him who exists,
> nor did they recognize the craftsman while paying heed
> to his works; . . .
> If through delight in the beauty of these things
> men assumed them to be gods,
> let them know how much better than these is their Lord,
> for the author of beauty created them.
> (Wisdom 13:1, 3; see Romans 1:20-23)

The downward move from the level of spiritual beauty to purely material beauty also tends to be reflected within the creature, and in particular, the woman. The representation of female beauty does not usually focus on the face in which the feelings and thoughts—in a word, the soul—of the woman are so clearly manifested, but focuses instead on other parts of the body, always the same parts. There are no more *Mona Lisa*'s in art, and at this point it seems doubtful that there will be any in the future.

Feminine beauty is entirely reduced to a means of seduction (sex appeal), to the grave detriment of women themselves, who end up being seen only in relationship to men as objects and not as persons.

4. Christ Has Redeemed Beauty

St. Paul wrote, "The creation was subjected to futility, not of its own will but by the will of him who subjected it in hope; . . . the creation itself will be set free from its bondage to decay and obtain the glorious liberty of the children of God" (Romans 8:20-21).

We could substitute the word "beauty" for "creation" in this text without changing the meaning of this affirmation in any way: "Beauty has been subjected to futility and waits to be set free." To save the world, beauty itself first needs to be redeemed. The redemption of Christ does, in fact, extend to beauty. Let us see how that happened.

A contrast between two statements about Christ is quite striking. On the one hand, he is seen as "the fairest of the sons of men" (Psalm 45:2), and "he reflects the glory of God" (Hebrews 1:3). On the other hand, the words of the Fourth Servant Song are applied to him in his passion: "He had no form or comeliness that we should look at him, and no beauty that we should desire him. . . . [He was] as one from whom men hide their faces" (Isaiah 53:2-3).

The explanation of this contrast is simple: Jesus redeemed beauty by depriving himself of it out of love. "Because he took flesh, he took, as it were, your hideousness, that is, your mortality, that he might adapt himself to you and correspond to you and arouse you to loving the beauty within. . . . 'He did not have attractiveness or comeliness' [cf. Isaiah 53:2], in order that he might give you attractiveness and comeliness."[13]

To understand this paradox we need to go back to the principle that Paul formulated at the beginning of 1 Corinthians: "For since, in the wisdom of God, the world did not know God through wisdom, it pleased God through the folly of what we preach to save those who believe" (1:21).

Applied to beauty, this means that since man is not capable of lifting himself up to the beauty of the Creator through the beauty of creatures, God changed his method, so to speak, and decided to reveal his beauty through the ignominy and the deformity of the cross and suffering, thus revealing his beauty through its opposite (*sub contraria specie*), as Luther might say. The attainment of beauty now comes about through the paschal mystery of death and resurrection.

The model and source of redeemed beauty is "the light of the knowledge of the glory of God in the face of Christ" (2 Corinthians 4:6). Beauty is no longer the abstract "splendor of truth,"[14] as Plato defined it, but is, concretely, the splendor of Christ (even if the two coincide since he himself is the Truth). Even Beauty was incarnated!

What differentiates this redeemed beauty from every other type of beauty, including bodily beauty? It is that this beauty comes from within, that it has its expression—but not its origin—in the body. The human body becomes the "sacrament" of beauty, i.e., its sign, its manifestation, its transparent expression, but not its ultimate source. It is not an opaque screen on which the light shines, but a window that lets light through.

It sometimes happens that the faces of contemplative nuns bring this mystery closer to us. We see nothing except faces and eyes, often looking down, yet the exclamation most often heard from those who have had such an encounter for the first time is "What faces! What light! What beauty!" We can say of them what Paul Claudel said about a young girl in one of his plays: "Other people's eyes absorb light; yours radiate it."[15] It is above all in the faces of children (at least those who have been fortunate enough to grow up in a healthy environment) that we see this beauty that emanates from innocence and purity of heart.

5. Participating in the Redemption of Beauty

How can we actively participate in this redemption of beauty? Christ, as I said, has redeemed beauty in the paschal mystery through its opposite, allowing himself to be stripped of every beauty. He has proclaimed that there is something superior to the very *love of beauty,* and it is *the beauty of love!*

What does all this mean for us? Should we renounce seeking and enjoying created beauty in this world, and most of all the beauty of the human body, as we await the transfiguration of our bodies in the final resurrection? No, created beauty is meant to embellish this life and not the future life, which will have its own beauty. A text from Vatican II speaks of the need for all human acts and values to "be purified and perfected by the power of Christ's cross," and concludes,

> For, redeemed by Christ and made a new creature in the Holy Spirit, man is able to love the things themselves created by God, and ought to do so. He can receive them from God, and respect and reverence them as flowing constantly from the hand of God. Grateful to his Benefactor for these creatures, using and enjoying them in detachment and liberty of spirit, man is led forward into a true possession of the world, as having nothing, yet possessing all things. [See 2 Corinthians 6:10][16]

Francis of Assisi is the most successful role model of this way of relating to creation. The saint of radical poverty is also the one who sang the beauty of creation in the most rapturous way. In his "Canticle," Brother Sun is "beautiful"; the stars are "precious and beautiful"; Brother Fire is "beautiful."[17] The most extraordinary thing is that Francis sang of the beauty of creatures when he could no longer see them, since by then he was almost blind, and the very light of the sun caused unspeakable pain to his eyes. Having renounced everything, he was able to rejoice in everything.

We can, then, enjoy created beauty if we also accept the cross that redeems it. And the cross of beauty does not entail some kind of strange suffering: it is love, and all that love requires is faithfulness, respect for others, submission to God, and the meaning of life—in other words, sacrifice and renunciation.

The redemption of beauty inevitably happens through a

choice now. Blaise Pascal, the French philosopher, said that there are three orders or categories of greatness: the order of bodies and material things, the order of intelligence and genius, and the order of holiness. Strength, physical beauty, and material wealth belong to the first order; genius, science, and art belong to the second; goodness, holiness, and grace belong to the third. (An analogous distinction occurs with Kierkegaard's three stages: aesthetic, philosophical, and religious.)

Between each of these three orders and the next one there is a qualitative difference that is almost infinite. The fact that a *genius* is rich or poor, beautiful or ugly, does not add or subtract anything, because that person's greatness is on a different and superior level. (The poetry of Giacomo Leopardi is very beautiful, even if his appearance was pitiable.) In the same way, the fact that a *saint* is strong or weak, rich or poor, highly intelligent or illiterate, does not add or subtract anything because that person's greatness is on a different and infinitely superior plane.[18]

Everything that Pascal says of *greatness* in general can also be said of *beauty*. There are three categories of beauty: physical or bodily beauty, intellectual and artistic beauty, and spiritual beauty. There is a large gap between each category. The beauty of the third category has a name that says it all: "grace." This word, which is a synonym for beauty, appeal, fascination, is also the word that applies to the interior beauty of the soul. (The root for "grace," *charis,* is the same one from which the Italian *carme,* the French *charme,* and English "charm" derive.)

"God's better beauty, grace," said one poet.[19] Nothing in the world—whether a spectacle of nature or a work of art—speaks to us as directly of divine beauty as grace does; it is not just a pale reflection of, but a direct "participation" in that beauty.

St. Teresa of Avila once saw the splendor of a soul in grace and compares it to a diamond that reflects light in every direction,[20] and St. Catherine of Siena says, "If you could see the beauty of a rational soul . . . there is nothing in this world that can compare with such beauty."[21]

The move from one category of beauty to the next-higher one—from external beauty to internal beauty and then to the transcendent beauty of grace—does not occur in a spontaneous and easy way. It requires an *ascesis* ("discipline") and, with regard to beauty in particular, an asceticism of the eyes. Ludwig Feuerbach said that people are what they eat; in our current culture wholly dominated by images, perhaps we need to say that people are what they look at.

St. Augustine was not embarrassed to reveal the struggle he had with this issue, and it occurred not in his youth but when he was a bishop. He describes the innumerable lusts of the eyes that are multiplied through the things that people produce (clothes, items, pictures, sculptures) and adds, "I say all these things and recognize their truth, yet still I snag my steps on these beautiful objects. . . . I am miserably caught, but you mercifully extricate me, sometimes without my being aware of it, when I am only lightly entangled, but sometimes painfully because I am already stuck fast."[22]

I do not know what Augustine would say if he were alive today after the invention of films, television, magazines, and the Internet! Jesus said, "If your right eye causes you to sin, pluck it out and throw it away" (Matthew 5:29). And how can the eye sin except because of what it looks at?

More important, however, than closing one's eyes to false beauty is opening them to true beauty: contemplating Christ crucified and risen. St. John Climacus writes, "A chaste man is someone who has driven out bodily love by means of divine love, who has used heavenly fire to quench the fires of the flesh,"[23] that is, the attraction to created things is driven out by attraction to Christ.

When we feel ourselves wounded by images of "carnal" beauty, let us do what the Israelites did in the desert. When they were bitten by poisonous snakes, if they quickly ran to look at the serpent lifted up by Moses they were healed (see Numbers 21:4-9). We too need to run, without losing time wanting to know why or how at our age . . . (which only gives time for the poison to spread); we need to run to a crucifix and look at it with faith (see John 3:14-15). The image of Christ and, even more so, the host that contains him in the sacrament also exercise their sanctifying power simply through sight, if our looking is accompanied by faith. Let the healing enter where the wound entered—through the eyes!

A different mode, but a very important one, of participating in the paschal mystery of the redemption of beauty is, lastly, to turn our attention to those who, like Christ in his passion, "have no form or comeliness that we should look at them"—the poor, the crucified, the rejected of our day. Blessed Mother Teresa of Calcutta, holding in her arms, with infinite tenderness, a sick child or a dying person who was abandoned, took part—despite all her wrinkles—in this redeemed beauty that also redeems. It will not be, I repeat, *the love of beauty* that will save the world, but *the beauty of love*.

Our cities are full of ads for beauty treatments. I want to advertise one too. The prescription is not mine but comes from my friend Augustine: a person becomes beautiful by loving

God. An ugly man does not become handsome because he loves a beautiful woman, but what is impossible on a physical level is possible on a spiritual level: "Our soul, my brothers, is hideous because of iniquity; by loving God it is made beautiful. . . . The more love increases in you, the more beauty increases."[24] A person becomes what he or she loves!

6. Bearing Witness to Beauty

I said at the outset that the problem of beauty is important not only for our spiritual lives but also with regard to the *proclamation* of the gospel. How do we evangelize through beauty?

Since Paul's time, two somewhat opposite methods have been laid out. The first, recasting what the apostle says about wisdom, could be formulated this way: "Today people seek beauty, but we preach Christ crucified who has neither splendor nor beauty" (see 1 Corinthians 1:22-23).

The second way, again paraphrasing the apostle, could be said this way: "Among the lovers of beauty, we too speak of beauty, although it is not a beauty of this world but a divine beauty, which has remained hidden and which God decreed before the ages for our glorification" (see 1 Corinthians 2:6-7).

In the history of the church we see this dialectic method (*sic et non*, "yes and no") faithfully reproduced in relating to the worldly values of wisdom and beauty. Some, starting with Tertullian ("What does Athens have to do with Jerusalem?"[25]), have chosen to bear witness to a radical detachment from worldly beauty corrupted by sin. They make no concession to the aesthetic sense but choose poverty and a radical divestment of everything, including the extreme cases of ascetics who persisted in destroying the signs of physical beauty in themselves so as to focus on interior beauty, and of people who live as "Fools for Christ" (radical Christians in the Russian tradition). Others, by contrast, have chosen to bear witness to divine beauty through its reflections in creation, which has resulted in all the great flowering of Christian art, the splendor of liturgies, of architecture, and of music.

It is important that both approaches are encouraged in the church, since each is the necessary corrective for the other. But if we had to choose one of the two approaches, I think that it would be important today to insist—as in every other area—on dialogue more than on the contrast, i.e., presenting the image of true beauty to the world more than denouncing false beauty.

The Trinity with whom we began our meditation offers us the richest indicator about how to bear witness to true beauty. Trinitarian beauty is the beauty of relationship. We should, therefore, strive to make our relationships beautiful: male-female relationships (inside and outside of marriage), relationships among friends, among clergy and laypeople in the church, among members of a religious community, between superiors and those under them, between young and old. What makes a relationship beautiful—taught to us once again by the trinitarian model—is solely and only love.

Consecrated people have a special responsibility in this regard. They need to bear witness in today's world that religious and spiritual life in general is not primarily a renunciation of, or even worse, a disdain for this world but a prophetic proclamation of the "new heavens and a new earth in which righteousness dwells" (2 Peter 3:13). And with righteousness, beauty!

1. See Psuedo-Dionysius Areopagite, *The Divine Names*, IV, 7, in *The Divine Names and Mystical Theology*, trans. and intro. by John D. Jones (Milwaukee, WI: Marquette University Press, 1980), pp. 139–40. He considers the word "beauty" (*kalos*) to be a derivation of "to call" (*kaleo*) insofar as it is something that beckons, that draws.

2. Augustine, *Confessions*, XI, 14, vol. 1, trans. by Maria Boulding, OSB, in *The Works of St. Augustine*, ed. John E. Rotelle, OSA (Hyde Park, NY: New City Press, 1997), p. 295.

3. I developed some of the reflections that follow in a book coauthored with Cardinal Carlo Martini, *St. Francis and the Cross: Reflections on Suffering, Weakness and Joy* ([Ann Arbor, MI: Servant, n.d.], pp. 23–47). I would like to share them here with a larger audience, since that other book was meant especially for priests.

4. Psuedo-Dionysius Aeropagite, *Divine Names*, I, 4, p. 111.

5. Cardinal Godfried Danneels, in his meditation to the extraordinary Consistory, May 2001.

6. Fyodor Dostoevsky, *The Idiot*, III, 5, trans. by Henry and Olga Carlisle (New York: The New American Library, 199), p. 402.

7. Paul Evdokimov, *The Art of the Icon: A Theology of Beauty*, trans. by Fr. Steven Bigham (Redondo Beach, CA: Oakwood Publications, 1990), p. 38.

8. Arthur Rimbaud, "Sisters of Charity" ["Soeurs de charité"], in *Rimbaud Complete*, trans. and intro. by Wyatt Mason (New York: Modern Library, 2002), p. 70; cf. also Charles Baudelaire, "The Vampire," trans. by George Dillon, in *The Flowers of Evil* [*Les fleurs du mal*] (Franklin Center, PA: The Franklin Library, 1977), pp. 50–51.

9. Fr. Serge Bulgakov, qtd. in Evdokimov, p. 88.

10. "Un soir, j'ai assis la Beauté sur mes genoux.—Et je l'ai trouvée amère.—Et je l'ai injuriée." Arthur Rimbaud, "A Season in Hell" ["Une saison en enfer"], *Arthur Rimbaud: Selected Poems and Letters*, trans. by Jeremy Harding and John Sturrock (New York: Penguin Books, 2004), p. 139.

11. Pico della Mirandola, *On the Dignity of Man*, intro. by Paul J. W. Miller, trans. by Charles Glenn Wallis (New York: Bobbs-Merrill Company, 1965), p. 5.

12. Augustine, *Confessions*, X, 27, p. 262.

13. St. Augustine, *Tractates on the First Epistle of John*, 9, 9, trans. by John W. Rettig, vol. 92 in *The Fathers of the Church* (Washington, DC: The Catholic University of America Press, 1995), pp. 258–59.

14. Plato, *The Republic*, trans. by Richard W. Sterling and William C. Scott (New York: W. W. Norton & Co., 1966), p. 198.

15. Paul Claudel, *The Humiliation of the Father* [*Le père humilié*], Act I, scene 1, in *Three Plays*, trans. by John Heard (Boston: John W. Luce Co., 1945), p. 155.

16. *Gaudium et spes* [Pastoral Constitution on the Church in the Modern World], 37, in *The Documents of Vatican II*, gen. ed. Walter M. Abbott, SJ, intro. by Cardinal Lawrence Shehan, trans. by Joseph Gallagher (New York: Herder and Herder Association Press, 1966), p. 235.

17. Francis of Assisi, "The Canticle of Brother Sun," in *Francis and Clare: The Complete Works*, pref. by John Vaughn, OFM, trans. and intro. by Regis J. Armstrong, OFM Cap, and Ignatius C. Brady, OFM (New York: Paulist Press, 1982), pp. 38–39.

18. Blaise Pascal, *Pensées*, 793, intro. by T. S. Eliot (Franklin, PA: The Franklin Library, 1979), pp. 237–38.

19. Gerard Manley Hopkins, "To What Serves Mortal Beauty?" in *The Poems of Gerard Manley Hopkins*, 4th ed., ed. by W. H. Gardner and N. H. MacKenzie (New York: Oxford University Press, 1967), p. 98.

20. See Teresa of Avila, *The Book of Her Life*, 40, 5, in *The Collected Works of St. Teresa of Avila*, vol. 1, trans. by Kieran Kavanaugh, OCD, and Otilio Rodriguez, OCD (Washington, DC: ICS Publications, 1976), p. 278.

21. Raymond of Capua, *The Life of St. Catherine of Siena*, trans. by George Lamb (New York: P. J. Kenedy, 1960), p. 138.

22. St. Augustine, *Confessions*, X, 34, p. 272.

23. John Climacus, *The Ladder of Divine Ascent*, Step 15, trans. by Kallistos Ware, trans. by Colm Luibheid and Norman Russel (New York: Paulist Press, 1982), p. 171.

24. St. Augustine, *Tractates on the First Epistle of John*, 9, 9, pp. 257–58.

25. From Tertullian, *De praescriptione haereticorum* [*The Prescription Against Heretics*], VII, 9.

Chapter 6

Gathered in the Name of the Father, the Son, and the Holy Spirit: CONTEMPLATING THE TRINITY TO BUILD COMMUNION

1. The Church Is Communion

This is the other important area in which there has to be commitment and planning on the part of the universal church and the particular churches: *the domain of communion (koinonia)*, which embodies and reveals the very essence of the mystery of the church. Communion is the fruit and demonstration of the love that springs from the heart of the Eternal Father and is poured out upon us through the Spirit that Jesus gives us (cf. Romans 5:5), to make us all "one heart and one soul" (Acts 4:32). It is in building this communion of love that the church appears as "sacrament," as the "sign and instrument of intimate union with God and of the unity of the human race."[1]

With these words from his apostolic letter *Novo millennio ineunte,* John Paul II has not only synthesized and summarized the doctrine of Vatican II on the church as communion but developed it further: "Communion is the fruit and demonstration

. . . of the essence of the mystery of the church," says the pope; the church, therefore, is communion.

We know that this was not always the way the church was understood. I have reread the notes on *De ecclesia*[2] I took during my theological studies, and I became aware of the enormous distance we have come in the last fifty years in this field. The church was not defined then as communion but as a "perfect society, immediately and freely instituted by Christ." In that view, the church is a society whose *material cause* was constituted by the multitude of its members, whose *formal cause* was the stable union of its members for the sake of the common good (this is how what we call "communion" today was thought of), whose *final cause* was eternal salvation, and whose *determinative principle* was authority.

The texts we were studying were written after Pius XII's encyclical *Mystici corporis,* and so they did address the fact that the church is also the mystical body of Christ and that these two perspectives are to be held closely together. But the nature of union between the two perspectives was not yet very clear, and the church, in its visible and social aspect, was not conceived as communion in its essence but as "a stratification of classes and of states, one more perfect than the other, descending from the summit to the base." This was the so-called pyramid concept of the church. *Hierarchy* preceded *communion,* leading to the various distinctions between the teaching church and the learning church, clergy and the faithful, religious and lay, and superiors and those submitted to them.

The emphasis today is instead on the fundamental equality of all the members of the people of God. All the faithful, regardless of their positions within the church, are part of this people because they share in mission and in the blessings of salvation. The unity of "Christian existence" and of mission precedes and is the basis for the distinctions of functions and ministries. The body of the church is a communion of brothers and sisters, structured according to a diversity of vocations in which the distinctions of functions and charisms do not negate the radical equality of the members.[3]

None of the constitutive elements of the church is essentially negated, but the overall alignment of these elements is profoundly new. (Perhaps it would be better to say "profoundly ancient," because this represents a return to the vision of the church prior to the controversy with Protestants that heavily influenced the theological reflection on the church for centuries.)

The pope adds in his letter,

While the wisdom of the law, by providing precise rules for participation, attests to the hierarchical structure of the Church and averts any temptation to arbitrariness or unjustified claims, the spirituality of communion, by prompting a trust and openness wholly in accord with the dignity and responsibility of every member of the People of God, supplies institutional reality with a soul.[4]

As we can see, the relationship between communion and hierarchy is inverted here; the hierarchy is now in service to communion, and not vice versa. Communion is seen as "the soul of the institution." Hierarchy is what will fade away, while communion is what will remain of the church for eternity.

Essentially it is a question of applying to the members of the same church what is said today about the relationship between

Christians of various churches: "The many areas which unite us . . . are unquestionably more numerous than those which divide us."[5] We are united in having one hope, one Lord, one faith, one baptism, and one God and Father, while the only thing that distinguishes us is that "some should be apostles, some prophets, some evangelists"; that is, that each one should exercise a particular and distinct function within the body (see Ephesians 4:4-11).

2. The Trinitarian Model

In this meditation I will focus on the theme of communion, insofar as communion, like everything else, finds its "high standard"[6] in the Trinity. Another way we can measure the distance that ecclesiology has come in this last half century is in fact precisely by looking at the source and the ultimate model of ecclesial communion. It is no longer just Christ and the union of humanity and divinity in him, flesh and Spirit, but something prior, the Trinity itself, as the beginning of the Letter to the Ephesians makes clear: God the Father has chosen us before the creation of the world; he has sent his Son to redeem us with his blood, and he has sealed us with the Holy Spirit (see Ephesians 1:3-14). The Trinity is like the matrix in which the church is formed. The Christological model is united with the trinitarian model and consequently with the pneumatological model.

"The Church," says *Lumen gentium,* using a quote from St. Cyprian, "shines forth as 'a people made one with the unity of the Father, the Son, and the Holy Spirit.'"[7] Henri de Lubac explained in a paper on the theology of Vatican II, "The Church is a mysterious extension of the Trinity in time, which not only prepares us for the unitive life but makes us already participate in it now. The church comes from the Trinity and is full of the Trinity."[8]

The pope refers to this perspective twice in his letter, saying, "A spirituality of communion indicates above all the heart's contemplation of the mystery of the Trinity dwelling in us, and whose light we must also be able to see shining on the face of the brothers and sisters around us,"[9] and also that the unity of Christ with the Father is "the well spring of the Church's unity and . . . the gift, which in him she will constantly receive until its mysterious fulfillment at the end of time."[10]

The Trinity is a mystery of communion at its very root. The members of the Trinity are not like people who enter into communion with one another through an event that joins them together, like the one that occurs in the church through baptism: rather, the divine Persons are in themselves, in their very nature, relationships of love, i.e., they are a communion.

This is where we can see the inexhaustible richness of Augustine's insight, perfected by St. Thomas Aquinas, in conceiving of the divine Persons as "subsistent relations." In simpler terms, "subsistent relations" means that a person does not *have* a relationship with another but *is* that relationship. This insight has been confirmed in modern times by Georg W. F. Hegel when he also conceived of a person as a being in relationship, "with the concept of person . . . [being] the recovery of self in the other."[11]

Being a communion of love, the Trinity has created man and woman in its image, that is, as beings in relationship. It is man and woman together who are the image of God.

The first biblical account highlights the sexual differences between man and woman. This is the first "otherness" that is experienced, the departure point on a road that will lead to discovering the other who is a neighbor and the Other par excellence, God. Paul Claudel explains why we need to start from this point:

> That man of pride! There was no other way to get him
> to understand his neighbour, to get inside his skin;
> There was no other way to get him to understand
> the dependence, the necessity and the need
> of another on him,
> . . . of that being [woman], different for no other reason
> save that it exists.[12]

But it is not the biological complementarity between man and woman per se that constitutes the image of God. God does not have the attributes and the experiences of sexual beings. There is a need, therefore, to go beyond the exclusivity of the male-female characteristics. The essential thing is that the human being does not remain alone. Human beings cannot become aware of their own "I" if there is not a gaze that turns toward them, a gaze that allows them at the same time to go out of themselves and to enter into intimacy—a gaze that also allows others to become conscious of themselves, to go out of their own "I" to entrust themselves fully in all their mystery. The gaze, the eye, is even more important than sex to enter into communion.

This helps us understand why those who cannot commit themselves to becoming a couple, through free choice or constrained by circumstances that are sometimes cruel, are not deprived of the dignity of being images of God. Christ did not marry, yet no one is more God's image or more perfectly human than he is! To say that a person is made in the image and likeness of God means that he or she is called to live "for" others, to become a gift, to be in relationship.

Friendship can also become a privileged place in which the image of God can become incarnate and in which one can learn to go out of oneself to open oneself to another.

3. The Church: An Image of the Trinity

But it is above all in relationship with the divine "Thou"—when God says, "I have loved you with an everlasting love" (Jeremiah 31:3)—that a person find his or her true worth and becomes conscious of his or her true "I" as a creaturely self. Prior to this, a person is lacking a criterion by which to be measured. According to Kierkegaard,

> A cattleman who . . . is a self directly before his cattle is a very low self, and similarly, a master who is a self directly before his slaves is actually no self—for in both cases, a criterion is lacking. The child who previously has had only his parents as a criterion becomes a self as an adult by getting the state as a criterion, but what an infinite accent falls on the self by having God as the criterion![13]

A living being, according to the Bible, is one to whom God speaks his word. It is, therefore, in the covenant, when a human being becomes God's conversation partner, that a human being fully becomes a "person." Here the means of communion par excellence is not a gaze (No one has seen God!) but the word.

The church belongs in this category because of the "new and everlasting covenant." The church is the reflection and image par excellence of the Trinity in time, because it is a communion of love, a communion in the Holy Spirit, between many people among themselves and with God.

In the period of the church fathers there was an animated discussion about the sense in which Christ is said by St. Paul to be "the image of the invisible God" (Colossians 1:15). The fathers of the Alexandrian School said that to truly reflect the model, the image of the invisible should also be invisible. Therefore, Christ is the image of God only insofar as he is the Word of God, i.e., in his divinity but not in his flesh. The fathers of the Antiochene School said it was absurd to think of an image that was invisible. If it is invisible, what kind of image is it, and for whom does it function as an image? Therefore, for them Christ is the image of God in his humanity, in his body.[14] Once the problem of the unity of the person of Christ, human and divine, was clarified at Chalcedon, it was finally possible to understand the original meaning of the Pauline affirmation: Christ is the image of God not only in just one aspect of his being, but in both. He could not be that image unless he were at the same time fully man and fully God.

This discussion sheds a unique light on the mystery of the church. It too is not an image of the Trinity only as a visible institution in its human dimension, because the visible cannot be an image of the invisible. Neither is it an image of the Trinity only due to its interior mystery of grace, because the invisible is not an image of anything, or, if it is an image, it is not an image that is useful for people or for the world. Therefore, we are also led by this path to affirm that the church is both "institution and mystery," a visible and invisible communion, or in a phrase used by Vatican Council II, "the universal sacrament of salvation."[15] A sacrament is both things together: a visible sign and an invisible reality.

Another point in the patristic discussion on Christ as the image of God sheds light on the mystery of ecclesial communion. In the polemic against the Arians, a distinction emerged between an artificial image, made of different kinds of material, and a natural image. The former would be the statue of a king made out of marble; the other would be the son of the king who is his living and natural image. Christ, who is the Son, is, therefore, a "perfect image" of the Father, or, as was added at Nicea, "consubstantial" with the Father.[16]

As I said, this sheds light on the mystery of ecclesial communion. The church is not consubstantial with God, but through grace its members "become partakers of the divine nature" (2 Peter 1:4). Ecclesial communion, then, is not an external imitation of, but a participation in the trinitarian communion among the divine Persons. It too is a living image, made of sons and daughters, not stones. What unites people in the church is the same bond that unites the Persons of the Trinity: the Holy Spirit. Ecclesial communion is *koinonia pneumatos*, "the fellowship of the Holy Spirit" (2 Corinthians 13:3) in the "Spirit of his Son" (Galatians 4:6).

What does a son desire more than anything? He certainly does not want his father and mother to love him separately. Unfortunately, it often happens that a husband and wife no longer love one another, and then each one channels his or her own love toward the son, perhaps in an attempt to attach him to themselves. But instead of making him happy, this only makes the son feel unhappy and insecure. What he secretly wants is for his father and mother to love each other and to include him in that love. He knows that he was born out of that love, and he feels torn apart if that love is missing. He does not want to be loved with a different love.

But here is the wonderful news: the three divine Persons love each other with an infinite love, and they allow us to enter into their love and make us participants in it. The Father loves us with the love with which he loves the Son, and we can love him with the love with which the Son returns that love, that is, "in the Holy Spirit." In this way we are able to interpret Psalm 36:9 in the light of Christian revelation: "They feast on the abundance of thy house, and thou givest them drink from the river of thy delights."

4. The Great Communion and Small Communions

This revelation invites us to an ecclesial examination of conscience. Called to the "great communion," we cannot let ourselves fall back into factions, parties, and other small human communions. Saint Paul also invites us, in his own way, to "aim high": "So let no one boast of men. For all things are yours, whether Paul or Apollos or Cephas or the world or life or death or the present or the future, all are yours; and you are Christ's; and Christ is God's" (1 Corinthians 3:21-23).

We know what caused this animated exhortation by Paul to the Corinthians: "For it has been reported to me by Chloe's people that there is quarreling among you, my brethren. What I mean is that each one of you says, 'I belong to Paul,' or 'I belong to Apollos,' or 'I belong to Cephas,' or 'I belong to Christ.' Is Christ divided?" (1 Corinthians 1:11-13).

Obviously, smaller communions based on common sentiments, ideals, or spirit are not to be excluded, but they should always exist within the great communion, never to its detriment or in opposition to it. If there must be opposition, this cannot be dictated by personal motives and interests but must occur in search of a more profound and wider communion. This is the reason Paul opposed Peter in Antioch, and the final result was not a wound but an enlargement of the communion to include the pagans.

There are not, unfortunately, certain criteria that can tell us in advance if something is a good or bad "rift." The only rule is the one Paul gave for eucharistic communion: *probet autem seipsum homo,* let each person examine himself or herself and the motives that guide them (see 1 Corinthians 11:28). If people are not able to examine themselves or allow themselves to be questioned by others, then others—the communion of the church—will test them. The church is like water: it "weighs" the bodies that fall into it. Those that have solidity and substance sink down into the water's depths, perhaps slowly, but the water receives them. Those that are empty and lack substance are pushed back up to the surface.

St. Paul says in one text that we can build on the foundation that is Christ "with gold, silver, precious stones, wood, hay, straw, . . . and the fire will test what sort of work each one has done" (1 Corinthians 3:12-13). Most often, time is the fire that tests the works. Those who first fought for the idea of the church as communion at Vatican II seemed at the time to break communion; now we know that they were actually building communion. The opposite must be said about some others. One fact that has always marked true prophets and true builders of communion has been their willingness to obey.

5. A Spirituality of Communion

The pope's letter exhorts us to build a spirituality of communion, to move from doctrinal discussions and clarifications to actual practice:

> Before making practical plans, we need *to promote a spirituality of communion,* making it the guiding principle of education wherever individuals and Christians are formed, wherever ministers of the altar, consecrated persons, and pastoral workers are trained, wherever families and communities are being built up.[17]

There is no spirituality without a corresponding *ascesis* ("discipline"). We need then to practice an *ascesis* of communion. In this case as well, the *ascesis* will consist above all in a "removal" (of obstacles). Ecclesial communion, in the theological sense, is more objective than subjective. In other words, it is not something that we construct; it is a sharing in the objective benefits of salvation—sacraments and charisms—that are summed up in the gift of the Holy Spirit.

Our fundamental task with regard to communion is not, then, to add something to it, but to remove the obstacles that impede the free movement of the Spirit in the organism of the church. We know the danger that obstructions, emboli, and constrictions of veins can have in the human body. . . .

The most dangerous obstruction, the one from which all the others come, has a specific name: it is a name in Italian that is almost identical to *Dio* ("God") but is actually his worst enemy: *io* ("I"), egotism. The text of the pope's letter refers to it: "A spirituality of communion means, finally, to know how to 'make room' for our brothers and sisters, bearing 'each other's burdens' (Galatians 6:2) and resisting the selfish temptations which constantly beset us and provoke competition, careerism, distrust, and jealousy."[18]

This is what caused the first break in the communion between God and human beings, between man and woman. St. Augustine describes what happens in that deadly circumstance with the term *curvitas* ("crookedness"): a person retreats into himself or herself and goes from being "straight" to being "bent," from being open and oriented to others as God planned, to being "closed" in on oneself. A healthy love of self that spurs people to find themselves by giving themselves to others, *amor socialis*, is transformed into an exclusive love of self, *amor privatus*. It is that wrong kind of *amor sui* ("self-love") by which Babylon, the city of Satan, is built throughout history.

The prayer the church lifts up to God in one of the prefaces for Lent resounds very appropriately here: "You ask us to express our thanks by self-denial. We are to master our sinfulness [egotism] and conquer our pride. We are to show to those in need your goodness to ourselves."[19] Every small victory over egotism becomes a stone with which we help construct the house of God that is ecclesial communion.

One good spiritual exercise is to defend the brother or sister with whom I am in discord in the tribunal of my heart. I become aware that I am making a case, taking someone to court inside myself. I take a determined stand against myself, I give up rehearsing all my arguments, and I try to put myself in the other person's shoes to understand his or her reasoning and what that person could say to me. I shout to myself, as they do in ecclesiastical tribunals: *Audiatur et altera pars*, "Now let the other side be heard."

We all have situations in which we can practice this. Communion is formed by concentric circles, starting with the most intimate—our own hearts—then moving out to the couple, the family, our church, all the churches, and ending with the largest circle of all humanity. One circle that is important for those of us who are religious is our own order. Many traditional religious orders have, somewhat like the universal church, stories of division, reform, and counter-reform in the past that have left their mark.

Today we can joyfully proclaim to the church that, following its example, we are committing ourselves to the healing of memories, the older orders collaborating among ourselves and with the new "forms of association" that the pope calls in his letter "a true 'springtime of the Spirit.'"[20] In brief, we are committed to building communion. All the jokes that once circulated about the rivalry between Dominicans and Franciscans, between Jesuits and Capuchins are no longer true. . . .

There is a highly symbolic biblical text that can inspire significant gestures of reconciliation and communion. It is the passage where God tells Ezekiel to take two sticks and to write on one, "For Judah, and the children of Israel associated with him," and to write on the other, "For Joseph (the stick of Ephraim) and all the house of Israel associated with him" (see Ezekiel 37:15-19). I once addressed the superiors of all the different Franciscan communities in Italy who were meeting precisely to promote initiatives for collaboration. I finished by reading this passage from the Bible. We did not have sticks close at hand, but we Franciscans did have one thing in common: the Franciscan cord.

Taking the cord of a Friar Minor, of a Conventual, of a Capuchin, and of a Third Order Franciscan, we unthreaded them and made a cord of four strands that each of us held tightly in our hand, like a chain, to express our desire for communion. (Augustinians, Dominicans, Carmelites, and others could, if they wish, do the same thing using their cinctures!)

1. Pope John Paul II, *Novo millennio ineunte* [At the Beginning of the New Millennium], 42 (Boston: Pauline Books and Media, 2001), p. 55.

2. "Concerning the Church," a standard curriculum topic in seminaries.

3. See Antonio Acerbi, *Due ecclesiologie: Ecclesiologia guiridica ed ecclesiologia di comunione nella "Lumen gentium"* (*Two Ecclesiologies: Juridical Ecclesiology and the Ecclesiology of Communion in "Lumen gentium"*] (Bologna: Dehoniane, 1975), p. 510.

4. Pope John Paul II, 45, pp. 59–60.

5. Pope John Paul II, *Tertio millennio adveniente* [As the Third Millennium of the New Age Draws Near], 16 (Città del Vaticano: Libreria Editrice Vaticana, 1974), p. 21.

6. Pope John Paul II, *Novo millennio ineunte*, 31, p. 43.

7. *Lumen gentium* [Dogmatic Constitution on the Church], 4, in *The Documents of Vatican II*, gen. ed. Walter M. Abbott, SJ, intro. by Cardinal Lawrence Shehan, trans. ed. Joseph Gallagher (New York: Herder and Herder Association Press, 1966), p. 17.

8. Henri de Lubac, "Quid significet ecclesiam esse mysterium" ["What It Means That the Church Is a Mystery"], in *Acta*

congressus internationalis: De theologia Concilii Vaticani II, Roma, 1968, p. 32.

9. Pope John Paul II, *Novo millennio ineunte,* 43, p. 57.

10. Pope John Paul II, *Novo millennio ineunte,* 48, p. 63.

11. See Bruno Forte's summary of Hegel's concept in *The Trinity as History: Saga of the Christian God,* trans. by Paul Rotondi, OFM (New York: Alba House, 1989), p. 73ff.

12. Paul Claudel, *The Satin Slipper* [*Le soulier de satin*], Third Day, scene viii, trans. by John O'Connor (New York: Sheed & Ward, 1945), p. 172.

13. Søren Kierkegaard, *The Sickness unto Death,* in *The Essential Kierkegaard,* ed. by Howard V. and Edna H. Hong (Princeton, NJ: Princeton University Press, 1995), p. 363.

14. See Raniero Cantalamessa, "Cristo 'Immagine di Dio': Le tradizioni patristiche su Colossesi 1:15" ["Christ as the 'Image of God': Patristic Traditions on Colossians 1:15"] in *Rivista di storia e letteratura religiosa,* XVI (1980 / 1–3) pp. 181–212; 345–80.

15. Pope John Paul II, *Novo millennio ineunte,* 48, p. 79.

16. See Hilary of Poitiers, *The Trinity,* VII, 37, trans. by Stephen McKenna, CSSR (New York: Fathers of the Church, Inc., 1954), p. 266.

17. Pope John Paul II, *Novo millennio ineunte,* 43, pp. 56–57.

18. Pope John Paul II, *Novo millennio ineunte,* 43, p. 57.

19. *The Sacramentary* (New York: Catholic Book Publishing, 1985), p. 393.

20. Pope John Paul II, *Novo millennio ineunte,* 46, p. 61.

Chapter 7

"We Will Arrive Where We Started":
Contemplating the Trinity
to Reach for Eternity

We shall not cease from exploration
And the end of our exploring
Will be to arrive where we started
And know the place for the first time.[1]

These verses from T. S. Eliot, the author of the famous play *Murder in the Cathedral,* only reveal all their beauty and profundity if they are applied to the Trinity. We must not grow tired of trying to explore the Trinity's mystery even if it infinitely surpasses our abilities. One day the exploration will cease, at least in its current form, and then we will discover that the place we have reached is the cradle in which we were born, but we will realize it only then.

We are like water that, after rising from the ocean and passing through the sky in the form of clouds, splashes back down between the river's banks and finds its rest in the sea again.

All the waters, in all the earth, are en route to the sea. Nothing can keep them from getting there. Men may build huge dams, there may be profound disturbances of the earth's surface that throw the river out of its course and force it to cut a new channel across a bed of granite, but at last the river will get to the sea. It may twist and turn, fall back on itself and start again, stumble over an infinite series of hindering rocks, but at last the river must answer the call of the sea. It is restless till it finds its rest in the sea.[2]

This is a very true image for our lives.

In this last reflection I want to speak about the Trinity as "the ocean of peace" toward which we flow, the "promised land" toward which we are journeying, the maternal womb that we reenter. We do not return unconsciously the way we left, but freely, joyfully, singing along the way the "psalms of ascent" that the pilgrims sang as they went up to Jerusalem:

I was glad when they said to me,
    "Let us go to the house of the LORD!" (Psalm 122:1)

1. The Trinity in the Resurrection of Christ

The hope of our final reunion with the Trinity is based on Christ's resurrection. By the mercy of God the Father, "we have been born anew to a living hope through the resurrection of Jesus Christ from the dead" (1 Peter 1:3).

There has been a lot of talk recently about the Trinity at the cross, but very little about the Trinity in the resurrection of Christ. According to some theologians, it is only at the cross, where the Father delivers the Son up to death, that the true revelation of the Trinity occurs.[3] The resurrection of Christ would not have any real intersection with the present world; it only assures us that there will be a redemption and a reversal in the eschatological fulfillment when the Son will hand over the kingdom to the Father—in other words, when all the redeemed will rise from the dead.[4] Only the long shadow of the cross, not yet illuminated by the light of the resurrection (except as a promise), extends over our present life. As I said in the second meditation, this is the weak aspect of the doctrine of the suffering of God—despite its richness—in the extreme version presented by some authors.

But in the resurrection of Christ something *happened* that does pertain to us now; it was not *proclaimed* or promised only for a distant future if Paul can already say that "we have been raised with Christ" (see Ephesians 2:6; Colossians 3:1). This may perhaps seem to be a subtle distinction, but it should be noted because it is extremely important. The transmutation of the sorrow of God into joy will not happen "only with the resurrection of the dead, the murdered and the gassed, only with the healing of those in despair who bear lifelong wounds. . . ."[5] It has already begun with the resurrection of Christ, which can be "viewed . . . as a unity with the present and the anticipated future."[6]

The resurrection of Christ is not merely a fact for apologetics intended to provide "solid proof" about Jesus; it is not primarily a demonstration of truth or power; it is not only the beginning of the church and of a new world. It is, first and foremost, the act of infinite tenderness by which the Father, after the terrible suffering of the passion, revived his Son from death by means of the Holy Spirit and made him Lord. For this reason, the resurrection is a trinitarian act just as much as the cross is.

The resurrection of Christ is the cry with which God, after holding back and putting up with violence for a long time, finally breaks his silence (see Isaiah 42:14). In the unfolding of events, human witnesses also play their part at a later time. The first-fruits of the resurrection were entirely accomplished between Jesus and the Father in the Holy Spirit in the most absolute intimacy. Everyone sees the *resurrected* Jesus, but no one sees him *rise from the dead.*

Christian tradition since the second century has placed on the lips of the risen Christ this cry of joy toward his Father: "I have risen, and I am still with thee," *Resurrexi et adhuc tecum sum* (see Psalm 3:5). The Father, for his part, cries out to the risen Jesus: "Thou art my Son, today I have begotten thee" (Acts of the Apostles 13:33; see Romans 1:4), as if the resurrection of Christ redoubled in him the joy of the eternal generation of the Word.

In his sermon at Pentecost, Peter applies the words of the psalm to Christ: "I keep the LORD always before me" (Psalm 16:8ff.). It is Jesus—not David—who is really speaking in this psalm; he is expressing his unshakeable trust that the Father would not abandon him in the tomb and that he would not see corruption (see Acts of the Apostles 2:24ff.).

The preferred term the New Testament authors use to express the event of the resurrection is the verb "raise" (*egeiro*), a transitive verb that points to the one who causes someone to rise, not to the one who rises. The Father, to express it in human terms, drew near to Jesus in the tomb just as someone here would gently draw near the crib of a child who is sick or sleeping, and awoke him from the sleep of death. The gospel tells us that Jesus one day came upon the casket of a young man who had died and cried out, "Young man, I say to you, arise," and the young man sat up, and Jesus returned him to his mother (see Luke 7:14). Now it is the Father who comes near the tomb of Jesus and cries out, "Son, I say to you, arise!" and Jesus sits up and arises.

The action of the Father in the resurrection is the source of the greatest hope for us, because it declares in advance what he will one day also do for us.

The action of the Spirit is just as evident in the resurrection. St. Paul says that through the resurrection Jesus was designated the Son of God in power "according to the Spirit of holiness," i.e., the Holy Spirit (see Romans 1:4). Jesus was "vindicated in the Spirit" (1 Timothy 3:16), declared to be justified and glorified in the Spirit. He was put to death in the flesh but "made alive in the Spirit," and still "in the Spirit" he went to the spirits in hell to announce salvation (see 1 Peter 3:18ff.).

The resurrection of Christ happened as predicted in the prophecy of the dry bones, which finds its pattern of fulfillment in him: "Behold, I will open your graves, and raise you from your graves, O my people; . . . And I will put my Spirit within you, and you shall live" (Ezekiel 37:12, 14). The Father made the Holy Spirit enter into Jesus, he returned to life, and the tomb was opened, unable to contain so much life.

This activity of the Holy Spirit in the resurrection of Christ is also a fountain of joy and hope for us. Scripture assures us that this will also happen to us: "If the Spirit of him who raised Jesus from the dead dwells in you, he who raised Christ Jesus from the dead will give life to your mortal bodies also through his Spirit which dwells in you" (Romans 8:11).

Not just the cross, then, but the resurrection is also a trinitarian event. Applying what happens within the Trinity to that which it does *ad extra* ("outside") in history, we can say that the Father is the one who resurrects, the Son is the resurrected one, and the Holy Spirit is the resurrection itself.

2. *Totaliter aliter!* ("Completely Different!")

We also need to integrate the Christological model with the trinitarian model when it comes to the eschatological dimension of the church. Eschatology is not just an expectation of the return of Christ; it is also a reunion with the Trinity, the return of creatures to God (*reditus creaturarum ad Deum*); it is "to arrive where we started." The idea of Christ's "return" at the end of time or of his "second coming" can become ambiguous if it leads us to think that the final goal of history is just here on earth once Christ has returned in glory.

Jesus said, "And when I go and prepare a place for you, I will come again and will take you to myself, that where I am you may be also" (John 14:2-3). That is the real final act in history: not the return of Christ but our entry with him into the Father's house. St. Paul also sees the conclusion of history as the moment in which Christ "delivers the kingdom to God the Father" (1 Corinthians 15:24) so that God "may be everything to every one" (15:28). ("Every one" means "all those who will have consented to submit themselves to him.")

At this point the question spontaneously arises, What will we do from this point on? Won't it be boring to spend all eternity with the same three Persons, even if they are divine? We could answer with another question: is it ever boring to enjoy feeling wonderful? People get bored of everything except "feeling wonderful," and eternity brings "infinite well-being."

We could ask lovers if they are ever bored of being together. When we happen to experience a moment of the most intense pure joy, don't we want it to last forever and never end? Those times do not last forever here below, because nothing here can satisfy indefinitely. Things are different with God. Our minds will find Truth and Beauty in him that we will never finish contemplating, and our hearts will find the Good that we will never tire of enjoying.

Something from modern science can help us understand this. Astronomers tell us that there are billions of galaxies, formed by billions of stars that are thousands of light years from one another. Scientists can only talk about that universe mathematically without being able to imagine it, and they know that they will never be able to finish exploring it. So will we ever finish exploring the One who created and contains that universe?

Augustine ended his treatise on the Trinity by saying, "So when we do attain to you, there will be an end to these many things which we say and do not attain, and you will remain one, yet all in all, and we shall say one thing praising you in unison, even ourselves being also made one in you."[7]

And thus it is clear that we have not really succeeded in saying anything. The best answer to the question "What will our life be like with the Trinity?" is found in a legend narrated by a modern German author. In a medieval monastery there were two monks, Rufus and Rufinus, who had a deep friendship. They spent all their free time trying to imagine and describe what eternal life would be like in the heavenly Jerusalem. Rufus was a builder, so he imagined it as a city with golden doors studded with precious stones; Rufinus was an organist, so he imagined it as full of heavenly melodies.

They ended up making a pact that whichever of them died first would return the following night to reassure the other that things were indeed as they had imagined. One word would do. If things were as they had imagined, he would simply say *Tali-*

ter! ("Exactly!"). If things were different—but this seemed completely impossible—he would say, *Aliter!* ("Different!").

One night while he was playing the organ, Rufinus died of a heart attack. His friend stayed awake anxiously all night, but nothing. He kept vigil and fasted for weeks and months, but nothing. Finally on the anniversary of his death, Rufinus entered his friend's cell at night in a circle of light. Seeing that Rufinus was silent, Rufus—sure of an affirmative answer—asked his friend, "*Taliter?* That's right isn't it?" But his friend shook his head no. Desperate, Rufus cried out, "*Aliter!* Different?" Again his friend shook his head no.

Finally his silent friend breathed forth only two words: "*Totaliter aliter*—Completely different." Rufus understood in a flash that heaven was infinitely more than what they had imagined and could not be described. He also died shortly after because of his desire to go there.[8] This story is a legend, but its content is nevertheless biblical:

> No eye has seen, nor ear heard,
> nor the heart of man conceived,
> what God has prepared for those who love him.
> (see 1 Corinthians 2:9)

3. Sojourners and Strangers

Let us come back to earth for a moment. When someone wants to cross a body of water, the most important thing is not to stand on the bank and strain to see what is on the opposite shore, but to board the ship that sails to that other shore. So too for us, the most important thing is not to speculate about what our life with the Trinity will be like, but to do the things that we know will bring us to it.

In his first epistle, John tells us, "And every one who thus hopes in him purifies himself" (1 John 3:3). I would like to mention one purification in particular suggested by the topic we are dealing with: purification of our attitude toward this world, of our relationship to it. We know how St. Paul conceives of this relationship:

> I mean brethren, the appointed time has grown very short; from now on, let those who have wives live as though they had none, and those who mourn as though they were not mourning, and those who rejoice as though they were not rejoicing, and those who buy as though they had no goods, and those who deal with the world as though they had no dealings with it. For the form of this world is passing away. (1 Corinthians 7:29-31)

"As though they did not . . . and were not." The liturgy in Lent often returns to that theme. I quote once again from a Lenten preface:

> This great season of grace is your gift to your family
>   to renew us in spirit.
> You give us strength to purify our hearts,
>   to control our desires,
>   and so to serve you in freedom.
> You teach us how to live in this passing world
>   with our heart set on the world that will never end.[9]

To have our hearts "set on" means to have them "oriented," and that word implies a turning toward the East, which is how Christian churches are built. But this instance deals with a special orientation—not toward the East but upward.

Let us go back to what Scripture tells us about our life here below as sojourners and strangers. A sojourner never puts down roots, never gets too attached to what is seen or encountered; that person has a destination and is always moving in that direction. That person closes his or her eyes, if necessary, to avoid being distracted, just as Ulysses had his men plug their ears so that they would not be drawn off course by the Sirens that they would meet along their way. . . .

We should all be "parishioners," and the whole church should be one large "parish." Let me explain. What did the term "parish" originally mean? In Acts of the Apostles we read that Israel was in exile in the land of Egypt (see 13:17). The Greek word that is translated as "exile" in modern translations was originally the word for "parish" (*paroikia*). Elsewhere we read that Abraham, by faith, lived his life as a sojourner and a stranger (see Genesis 15:13; Hebrews 11:9). In 1 Peter 1:17 we read, "Conduct yourselves with fear throughout the time of your exile"—literally, "in the time of your parish"—and again he says, "I beseech you as aliens and exiles to abstain from the passions of the flesh" (1 Peter 2:11)—literally, "I beseech you as parishioners to abstain from the passions of the flesh."

What do the words *paroikia* and *paroikos* mean? Very simply, *para* is a preposition meaning "alongside," and *oikos* is a noun that means "dwelling place." A "parishioner," then, is one who lives alongside or near, not inside but on the periphery. From here the word came to mean someone who lived in a place for a little while, someone who was passing through, or someone who was exiled from the homeland.

At the beginning this was the fundamental understanding of Christian identity. This is expressed, for instance, in the letters exchanged among the earliest Christian communities. The letter of Pope Saint Clement to the church in Corinth begins this way: "The church of God which sojourns [literally, which is "in parish"] in Rome to the church of God which sojourns in Corinth."[10] The epistle to Diognetus describes Christians this way: "They live in their own countries, but only as aliens [*paroikos!*]; they participate in everything as citizens and endure everything as foreigners. Every foreign country is their fatherland, and every fatherland is foreign."[11]

There is, therefore, an awareness of the alien nature of the world that is part of the very essence of Christian life. The definition that the ancients gave to a monk can also apply—with appropriate distinctions—to every Christian: "A monk is someone who is separated from all and united to all."[12] A person united to the world is useful to it insofar as he or she is separated from it in thinking and acting.

This approach does not imply any kind of desire to die early; rather, it implies the decision to "live for the Lord." We are familiar with the words of the elderly St. Martin de Tours: "If God finds that I can still be of use to his people, I do not at all refuse to work and to suffer longer."[13]

4. The Last Passover

Passover offers us the most helpful illustration of this purification of our relationship to the world. John has given us a new definition of the Passover after Christ: "to depart out of this world to the Father" (John 13:1). The Middle Ages summarized the doctrine of the four senses of Scripture in this famous couplet:

> The Letter speaks of deeds; Allegory to faith;
> The Moral how to act; Anagogy to our destiny.[14]

Applying this to Passover, one medieval author says, with perfect logic,

> The Passover can have an historical, allegorical, moral, and anagogical significance. *Historically*, the Passover occurs when the avenging angel passed over Egypt; *allegorically*, when the church passes from unbelief to faith in baptism; morally, when the soul, through confession and contrition, passes from vice to virtue; *anagogically*, when we pass from the misery of this life to eternal joy.[15]

We need to rediscover this anagogical meaning of the Passover and of the whole Christian life. "Anagogical" means that which tends upward, toward the eternal Passover, the one that we will celebrate in the kingdom of the Father . . . "with ten thousand angels in a most perfect assembly and a most blessed exodus."[16] Revelation 19:9, describing eternal life as "the marriage supper of the Lamb" (*coenam Agni*), is saying precisely this, that it will be an eternal Passover feast. It will be the final and definitive Passover, because it will be a *passing over* to that which does not pass away.

In these meditations, I have tried to stammer out something about the mystery of the Most Holy Trinity. But I am sure that one day when we cross the threshold of the heavenly Jerusalem, the words that will come spontaneously to our lips will be the words of the monk to his friend: "*Totaliter aliter!* Completely different!"

1. T. S. Eliot, "Little Gidding," V, *Four Quartets*, in *The Complete Poems and Plays, 1909–1950* (New York: Harcourt, Brace & World, 1971), p. 145.

2. Howard Thurman, *Deep River: Reflections on the Religious Insight of Certain of the Negro Spirituals* (New York: Harper & Brothers, 1945), p. 73.

3. See Jürgen Moltmann, *The Crucified God: The Cross of Christ as the Foundation and Criticism of Christian Theology*, trans. by R. A. Wilson and John Bowden (New York: Harper & Row, 1973), p. 241ff.

4. Moltmann, p. 160ff.

5. Moltmann, p. 278.

6. Wolfhart Pannenberg, *Revelation as History*, trans. by David Granskou (New York: Macmillan, 1968), p. 84.

7. Augustine, *The Trinity*, XV, 51, trans. by Edmund Hill, OP, vol. 5 in *The Works of Saint Augustine*, ed. by John E. Rotelle, OSA (Brooklyn, NY: New City Press, 1991), p. 457.

8. Hans Franck, *Der Regenbogen, Siebenmalsieben Geshchicten* [*The Rainbow: Seven Times Seven Stories*] (Leipzig: Haessel, 1927).

9. "Second Lenten Preface," *The Sacramentary* (New York: Catholic Book Publishing Co., 1985), p. 391.

10. Clement of Rome, "Letter to the Corinthians," Greeting, in *The Apostolic Fathers*, trans. by J. B. Lightfoot and J. R. Harmer,

2nd ed. (Grand Rapids, MI: Baker Book House, 1989), p. 28.

11. "Epistle to Diognetus," 5, 5, in *The Apostolic Fathers*, trans. by J. B. Lightfoot and J. R. Harmer, 2nd ed. (Grand Rapids, MI: Baker Book House, 1989), p. 299.

12. Evagrios of Pontus, "On Preaching," 124, *Philokalia*, vol. 1, trans. by G. E. H. Palmer et al. (Boston: Faber and Faber, 1979), p. 69.

13. Martin de Tours, quoted in Omer Englebert, *The Lives of the Saints*, trans. by Christopher and Anne Fremantle (New York: David McKay Co., 1951), p. 429. Official Latin of the feast: "*Si adhuc populo tuo sum necessarius, non recuso laborem.*"

14. "*Littera gesta docet, quid credas allegoria. / Moralis quid agas, quo tendas anagogia*"; attributed to Augustine of Dacia, *Rotulus pugillaris*, I; see *Catechism of the Catholic Church*, 118, p. 33.

15. Sicardus of Cremona, *Mitrale*, VI, 15 (PL 213), p. 543.

16. Origen, *Commentary on John*, X, 111, trans. by Ronald E. Heine, vol. 80 in *The Fathers of the Church* (Washington, DC: The Catholic University of America Press, 1989), p. 279.